THE DARK AGE
OF TANKS

THE DARK AGE OF TANKS

BRITAIN'S LOST ARMOUR, 1945–1970

DAVID LISTER

Pen & Sword
MILITARY

AN IMPRINT OF PEN & SWORD BOOKS LTD.
YORKSHIRE – PHILADELPHIA

First published in Great Britain in 2020 by
PEN AND SWORD MILITARY
An imprint of
Pen & Sword Books Ltd
Yorkshire – Philadelphia

ISBN 978 1 52675 514 8

A CIP catalogue record for this book is available from the British Library.

Printed and bound in England by TJ International, Padstow, Cornwall, PL28 8RW
Typeset in Times New Roman 11.5/14 by
Aura Technology and Software Services, India

Pen & Sword Books Limited incorporates the imprints of Atlas, Archaeology,
Aviation, Discovery, Family History, Fiction, History, Maritime, Military, Military
Classics, Politics, Select, Transport, True Crime, Air World, Frontline Publishing,
Leo Cooper, Remember When, Seaforth Publishing, The Praetorian Press,
Wharncliffe Local History, Wharncliffe Transport, Wharncliffe True Crime and
White Owl.

For a complete list of Pen & Sword titles please contact
PEN & SWORD BOOKS LIMITED
47 Church Street, Barnsley, South Yorkshire, S70 2AS, England
E-mail: enquiries@pen-and-sword.co.uk
Website: www.pen-and-sword.co.uk

Or

PEN AND SWORD BOOKS
1950 Lawrence Rd, Havertown, PA 19083, USA
E-mail: Uspen-and-sword@casematepublishers.com
Website: www.penandswordbooks.com

Contents

Acknowledgements

My special thanks go to the following people who helped with this work, either as advisor, editor or someone with whom to discuss my findings. They are Andrew Hills, Ed Francis, Stan Lucian and Thomas Anderson.

The following individuals have provided images for this work, and I can only express my gratitude to them. They are Simon Parkinson, Ed Francis and artist William Byrd.

Help with research was carried out by Károly Németh, Ed Francis and Thomas Anderson.

I also held a competition, among my regular readers, to help name some of the chapters in this book. The winners of that are the following: Dominic Tolson, Denis Richard and Jeremy Rosenblad.

Introduction

Over the years, I have visited a number of archives looking for information about British armour development. At several of them, I have talked to the head librarian or curator of the collection, and all have had a common story. They tell of the absolutely dire state of the UK archives. Each has his own little story about how they have fought to save documents. One tells of how an unmarked brown envelope was left in their post box with a sheaf of tank documents and a note. Several tell of visiting an army installation and finding documents or models being thrown into a skip and they have to grab what they can, loading the stuff into their car. When they return the skip has gone, and what they had managed to save is all that remains of an irreplaceable collection that contained unknown wonders.

Other archives owned by private companies simply cannot be accessed. One has a heritage manager who is only interested in one small segment of the archive's contents, and all enquiries not relating to that small part get lost or mislaid. Other private companies just plain lie about the documents they hold, and then charge thousands of pounds for seeing the documents.

On top of all that, there is no one single source for all the documentation. There are hundreds of small museums, each with its own collection. Sometimes they will work out a deal with another organization and split the collection in a swap with other archives so that your plans to view documents evaporate weeks before you are due to visit.

It was even worse in the years following the Second World War. Great swathes of documents were just destroyed outright, and we lost so much. David Wiley, the Tank Museum chief librarian, described the thirty years after the Second World War as the 'Dark Age of Tanks'. This is solely because so much knowledge was lost, and so little of what remains has been viewed as part of the larger whole.

This work is an attempt to fill in the blanks, to take a look at how the British projects developed, and shed some light on the period. It should, however, by no means be taken as the detailed truth. As more work on the subject is done, I fully expect that some of what I write in the following pages will be altered. Consider this work as a jumping-off point; a primer, if you will. Maybe a first weak lamp illuminating the 'Dark Age of Tanks'...

David Lister
www.historylisty.com
www.facebook.com/historylisty

PART 1

Armour of the Line

Chapter 1

The End

Victory! After six years of struggle, at 1000 hours on 21 July, the 25-pounders of the 7th Armoured Division started to fire. This salvo was the signal for the opening of the British Victory in Europe parade. Row after row of armour drove past the viewing stand. Taking the salute were Prime Minister Winston Churchill and Field Marshal Montgomery. Britain had started the war with a vast array of tank classifications, such as light cruiser, cruiser, battlecruiser, heavy cruiser, light and infantry tanks. Along with this vast selection of types, the General Staff had an utterly baffling tank policy and doctrine. However, the white-hot need of the Second World War had burned the preconceived notions away to just two classes: cruiser and infantry. Even then, the cruiser class was nebulous as the British had a vast number of Sherman tanks in service that did not strictly fit British classifications.

Those years after the Second World War were a critical time. First, the army had to boil all its hard-won experience down into a doctrine and arm itself for new conflicts. A hint of those new enemies came in September 1945, when the four major Allies held a joint victory parade in Berlin to mark the end of the war. Fifty-two brand new IS-3s of the Soviet 2nd Guards Tank Army took part in the spectacle. The IS-3 caused a lot of concern among the Western Allies, and for many years after it was the benchmark against which all British tanks were compared. As well as the shock of the Soviet weapons the Allies were potentially facing, with the war now over, a cut in weapons production and the financial costs for defence spending came about and the Treasury became a new opponent.

At the end of the war, the British forces had some 2,077 tanks, split between Cromwells, Comets and Churchills, as well as an unknown number of tanks procured from the United States. By October 1946 this, plus the final wartime production contracts output, amounted to enough

Soviet IS-3s feed into the bottom of the Charlottenburger Chaussee (now Strasse des 17. Juni), heading towards the Brandenburg Gate. The street was the site of the victory parade on 17 September and was the first glimpse of the new face of Soviet armoured warfare.

tanks to equip the entirety of the shrinking RAC (Royal Armoured Corps) with tanks of British origin and leave a reserve of 50 per cent of the force.

Field Marshal Montgomery's idea was to replace all these multitudes of classes with one tank. The class was first referred to as the 'Capital tank' but would soon be termed the 'Universal tank'. Today, we would call this the Main Battle Tank (MBT).

Montgomery had begun to agitate for the universal tank in 1943 and, between 12 and 15 February of 1945, before the war had ended, the RAC held Operation FAIRY in Rome. The delegates comprised serving officers from the main British field units in the 8th Army, as well as Canadian and New Zealand formations, along with representatives from the War Office. This conference managed to sample the entire range of experience from the wartime UK armed forces and government, ranging from front-line soldier to the tank designer in the UK. One of the activities at this conference was the forming of four syndicates to consider the problem of the universal tank. Several lectures about the particulars of tank design were held, which included discussions at the end of each talk with the officers proposing their views on the subject. These views were often the result of hard-won combat experience. During these discussions, the conference delegates were questioned on various subjects such as if the attendees wanted an assault gun with a casemate, such as a 'Jagd-Churchill' or 'Jagd-Cromwell' with a 17-pounder gun, or maybe even a 3.7in gun, or a turreted tank. Another topic raised was if a weight of 60 tons was the upper limit for tank design. There was also a long look at the subject of secondary weapons, covering the .30 and .50 calibre machine guns and the 20mm cannon. These discussions also included the 15mm BESA machine gun, a weapon that had disappeared from British front-line use some years earlier. The 20mm was also quickly discounted due to its size and slow rate of fire. Also, the 20mm Polsten gun was singled out for some dislike due to its cocking mechanism, which was described as 'being beyond the ability of most men to work', and that it needed a special device that would cock it slowly. In its defence, it was identified as being the ideal weapon for use against anti-tank guns due to its light armour-piercing abilities and explosive shell. These contrary arguments might explain why the first Centurion tanks had a Polsten but almost immediately had it replaced with a 7.92mm BESA machine gun.

The first Centurion. On this Mk 1 one can clearly see the 20mm Polsten gun that came in for such dislike in Operation FAIRY. It should be noted that the opinions of the Polsten were likely due to the experience of the weapon in Cromwell AA tanks, not the Centurion. However, the animosity would likely remain and be the cause of the replacement of the 20mm with the BESA in subsequent Centurion variants.

After the discussions, the syndicates split off to design their ideal tank. When they were finished, their ideas were discussed by the conference. All the tanks came in between 50 to 60 tons. Syndicate one pretty much designed a Churchill Mk VIII, with an extra 50mm of frontal armour. In a change to contemporary thinking, the gunner doubled as the loader, and the top speed of 20mph was questioned by the experts in armour design who attended the conference. It was suggested that 10mph might be more realistic.

Syndicate two went for a 250mm armoured tank armed with a 3.7in gun. To power it to the requested 25mph the members suggested a petrol engine, although if science offered sufficient technological advances a diesel or even steam engine could be employed. Unsurprisingly, the last engine suggestion was firmly rejected by the senior officers who knew about engine technology.

Syndicate three is where things began to get a bit odd. They proposed a 105mm gun firing high-explosive anti-tank rounds, with a rifle-calibre coaxial machine gun. The hull gun was given as a 15mm BESA, and they wanted their tank to be fully submersible. While syndicate three did not get a complete specification down, they did better than syndicate four which said it had nothing new to advance.

Back in London, immediately after the war, the decision to equip the entirety of the RAC with Centurion tanks was taken. This choice was seen as a short-term solution. In the longer term, a new tank would be produced to replace the Centurion. This new tank would be equivalent to an improved Centurion tank, with a General Staff number of A.45. It was to be designed by the General Staff's vehicle design wing, and its plans would be available in 1947. After the A.45 was complete, the tank the RAC wanted for a major war, within the next twenty years, would be considered.

At the very start of 1946, Major General Raymond Briggs, who was the Director of the Royal Armoured Corps (DRAC), asked for a study of material in the press about the types of tank needed by the army. The resulting paper, entitled 'The Universal Tank', was written by L.C. Manners-Smith, and took some six months of work. The time taken was seen as a long period of time for such a short study but was partially down to a change in the terms of reference in March after a conference at Camberley. However, Manners-Smith was able to finish his report by the end of June and submitted it with a sense of a job well done. The report contained some startling conclusions which caused Major General Briggs to restrict access and generally suppress the distribution of it. The conclusions that DRAC railed against were the comments on needing the most armour that could be loaded onto the tank, mostly for morale purposes, and to the exclusion of reliability. Manners-Smith cited the fear of the German Tiger tank and the common occurrence of up-armouring tanks with track links and other junk later in the war during the European campaign. Against it, Major General Briggs was swayed, presumably, by the experience of British armour in the North African desert, where he felt morale was damaged by the poor reliability of the British tanks. Other points included the feeling that the report concentrated too much on anti-tank guns, both friendly and the enemy's, and not enough on the hypothetical tank dealing with enemy armour.

Oddly, the complaints Major General Briggs levelled at the report did not seem to extend to some of the more outlandish claims Manners-Smith made, such as the width of the tank potentially being up to 16ft. In comparison, a modern tank such as the Challenger 2, with side skirts on, is about 13ft. Because of this width, the tank was not meant to use transporters but drive everywhere on its tracks, which would cause damage to roads. Manners-Smith deemed this acceptable, apparently ignoring the knock-on effect this would have on the logistics tail that all armies have. In at least one of the copies of the report, these conclusions were underlined and exclamation marks added by the unknown reader.

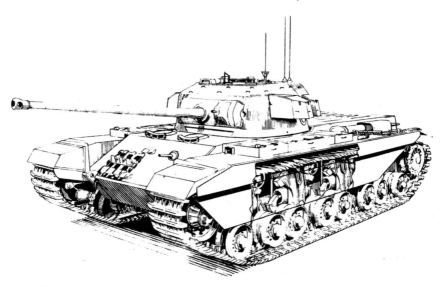

One of the first sketches of the A.45, with several differences. The most obvious of these is the ball mount for the hull machine gun, which would later be altered to the blister mount that would be a distinctive feature of later models.

THE END

When discussing other parts of the tank design, Manners-Smith was much more prophetic. For example, he said the upper weight limit of the tank could be as high as 70 tons. This prediction was based on a survey of the UK carried out during the Second World War in which every bridge in the country was inspected and given a bridge classification. From this, Manners-Smith was able to say that only occasional detours would be needed for a 70-ton tank, and he applied that standard to Europe.

Notable among the other suggestions in the report was one listing the importance of mobility, but not speed. While speed is a factor of mobility, the idea was that high-speed cross-country driving in a tank would cause injury to the crew, but the ability to maintain an adequate speed on any terrain would be of more use. The report points towards the 6th Guards Tank Brigade which, despite being equipped with Churchills, was able to keep pace with other armoured units equipped with faster vehicles. Further support for the report's conclusions can be drawn from the same unit, which managed to keep on advancing around Cleves in terrain that was so bad, due to the Germans flooding the area, that supplies had to be brought up to the Churchills in DUKW amphibians. One of the regiments of the 6th Guards, the 4th Coldstream, also held the record for the fastest advance of any armoured unit within the 21st Army Group. Even today, that legacy lives on in British armour. The Challenger 2 might not be the quickest MBT on the road, but it is one of the best cross-country performers in the world.

In mid-1946, a significant change took place, not just in the A.45 programme but across the British army. One of the changes was the removal of the pre-war British doctrine of Cruiser and Infantry tanks. In addition, the old system of General Staff numbers was replaced by the numbering system still in use today. The FV numbers had arrived. The first number denoted a tank's series, and then its sub-type in the series was indicated by the rest of the numbers. As the A.45 became the FV200 series, an example is the FV208, which was a bridge-layer. The 2 showed it was based on the FV200 chassis and the 08 that it was the eighth variant in the series. At this time there were a total of twelve FV200 series vehicles planned:

- FV201: Gun tank, with 20-pounder gun
- FV202: AVRE(T), with 6.5in BL gun
- FV203: AVRE(L)
- FV204: Flail gun tank

- FV205: Self-propelled medium anti-tank gun, armed with a proposed 4.5in gun
- FV206: Self-propelled medium artillery
- FV207: Self-propelled heavy artillery
- FV208: Bridge-layer
- FV209: Armoured recovery vehicle
- FV210: Tractor for heavy artillery
- FV211: Tractor for medium artillery
- FV212: Heavy armoured personnel carrier.

The FV200 got the 2-series number as the tracked vehicles were initially arranged by their weight, although this was just convenience when drawing up the new system. The FV300 series was a selection of small armoured vehicles based upon a lighter chassis up to about 20 tons in weight. Like the FV200, the FV300 had a range of vehicles on a standard chassis, including SPGs (self-propelled guns). The tanks themselves were light tanks, and the best anti-tank gun fitted to these light tanks was a 77mm gun. The project was officially cancelled in June 1952. However, the prototype continued running until 1954. The reason for this was that the parent company, Vickers, continued to develop the chassis and running gear and these designs would resurface for several years until finally being included in the FV400.

Precious little actually survives in the documents on the FV100 series. This designation seems to be just a placeholder number for future need. If the army ever suddenly found itself needing a super-heavy class of armoured tanks, then these numbers would have been used. The FV101 was meant to be an assault tank, while the FV102 was destined for a future super-heavy self-propelled anti-tank gun. They were weighted in

A side view of the FV300 mock-up, showing its maximum gun depression.

the 75 to 100-ton range, and the little work that was done with them seems to imply that they were based upon the A.39 Tortoise suspension. There is a rumour among tank historians of a Tortoise Mk II with a 1,000hp engine, and it may be that these are linked to the FV100 series. However, there is no definite proof. The only other hint was when Pickfords Ltd spent a lot of effort and time moving some of the six A.39 Tortoises that were built around the countryside in what was presumably a series of trials and studies on the movement of large armoured vehicles.

Returning to the FV200, the earlier list highlights that the flail-equipped version became a separate tank. Initially, all A.45s were to be able to be equipped with a flail attachment. This upgrade would have given the tank a width of some 16ft. The flail attachment would be directly linked to the A.45's power take-off but would limit it to a speed of just 1mph while flailing. In an attempt to try to reduce the width of the tank, there was a suggestion that fitting 24in instead of 32in tracks would reduce the width sufficiently. Such a change would have narrowed the outside dimension of the tank, but this was rejected. Making the flail a permanent part of the vehicle led to a much-needed decrease in the width of these mine-clearing vehicles. In addition, it allowed the fitting of specialist gearboxes to the power take-off, which allowed a faster flailing speed.

The Pickfords' public relations machine, knowing that such a huge tank would be sure to attract attention, felt that investing in some paint for the heavy duty trailer would offer a good return. Here one can see the size and engineering that went into the transporter. The rear axle with four huge wheels that run the entire width of the trailer should give some idea of the difficulties involved.

Chapter 2

A Tank For All

Details of the A.45's early years are shrouded in mystery. It is certain that the A.45 was designed by the Department for Tank Design (DTD) sometime around the end of 1944, as the Tank Board had a report submitted that the A.45 was under design, with the suspension and hull complete, in January 1945. The tank was described as the Infantry tank version of the A.41 Centurion. With the 1946 banishment of the concept of Infantry tanks, the tank was sufficiently advanced in its design to be adopted as the new Universal tank. The main differences between the A.45 and the Centurion were the suspension type and the sides of the tank being vertical instead of sloped as in the A.41. The A.45 was to be designed to cover a vast range of roles, such as being equipped as a flame-thrower, or with a flail device for mine-sweeping. The question of 'Why not just use a Centurion for all these roles?' was raised several times. Invariably, the answer would be that yes, the A.41 could be adapted; however, it would compromise too much. For example, the fitting of a flame gun to the Centurion had two options. The first was to mount the flame gun in a contraption on the driver's hatch, which would massively overwork the driver and would foul the turret and main gun. The other option was to drastically alter the hull, with a fifth man dedicated to manning a flame gun. This extra crewman would involve the removal of far too many rounds of main gun ammunition, as the Centurion's main ammo rack was in the same position as the hypothetical hull gunner would need to be. In the case of the Duplex Drive (DD) amphibious tank, the entire rear of the tank would need to be redesigned. In both examples, it was seen as much more straightforward, more uncomplicated and more cost-effective to design these features into the fabric of the tank from the start. The two tanks were so similar in design that the unarmoured hull used as a prototype for the A.41 was butchered to create a test bed for the A.45 by slicing it in half and adding a spacer behind the turret ring.

In addition, the A.45 was seen as a replacement for a variant of the A.43 Black Prince with a Meteor engine with a petrol injection system fitted. This engine would become known as the Meteorite. At this time, Sir George Nelson had offered to take over the design of the A.45 at English Electric due to a lack of capacity at DTD, and this offer was accepted.

As well as the differences in hull sides and the suspension, the complete A.45 had several other improvements such as wider tracks giving 2psi less ground pressure than a Centurion. The glacis armour was improved, being slightly thicker at 76mm and more sloped. The roof armour was also thickened, up to 32mm. The lower nose was 76mm. Skirts were about 6.5mm and the floor 20mm. The best-armoured part of the hull was 89mm thick and was the 'forehead' of the upper glacis, which connects to the roof.

The fighting compartment of the A.45 was larger than that of the Centurion and contained more ammunition and a co-driver. Both the driver and co-driver benefited from improved hatches that popped up and swung out, similar to the FV4201 Chieftain driver's hatch, instead of the

The business end of the FV200, clearly showing the details of the machine-gun blister and the sight unit for it.

vertically-opening door-style hatches used on an A.41. The Centurion-style hatches could be blocked by the turret and gun, preventing escape in an emergency. Another improvement for the driver was the episcopes. These were increased to wide-angle versions and mounted in the roof of the tank instead of being installed in the driver's hatch as on the Centurion. The co-driver's primary responsibility was to fire the hull machine gun. The earliest A.45 plans had a ball-mounted machine gun in the glacis plate, and this was later removed to improve the armour's integrity. The new location for the machine gun was installed in a blister over the left track. The blister had 70mm of armour and mounted a .30 calibre Browning machine gun, which was linked to a periscope sight. The controls were a set of handlebars with a trigger. The periscope was mounted to the handlebars and could be stowed when not in use. Moving the periscope to its stowed position would automatically close a dust cover over the outside optics as well.

In 1947, the engine was planned to be a V12 Meteor Mk XI manufactured by Rover that produced some 800hp. However, another document created at the same time says that the engine is a Meteor Mk II producing 860hp. The engine fed to a seven-speed gearbox made by David Brown Tractors, giving five forward and two reverse gears. Steering was a done by a Merritt-Brown contorted differential, and brakes were made by a company called Girling. These brakes came in two types. Both were internal expanding two leading shoe types. The difference between the two was the steering brakes had a mechanical interlock to prevent both being activated at the same time, while the main brakes did not.

To access the engine bay a series of doors was arranged on the roof of the hull, very similar to those used on a Centurion. When the General Staff required these doors to be increased in thickness to 17mm to provide protection against 5.5in air-bursting shells, the heavier doors were tested on a Centurion first. It was found that if the clearance between the turret and the hatches was made sufficient and an extra handle fitted, there would be no problems with the weight of the doors. There was also to be an auxiliary power unit fitted to provide electrical power without running the main engine.

The suspension was of the helical spring type, with four units per side. These were not identical, as the first and last units had two wheels in their return rollers while the middle pair of suspension units had a single wheel. Equally, the Newton and Bennett shock absorbers were only fitted to the leading and trailing units. The road wheels themselves were to be newly-designed resilient solid wheels. Three manufacturers were asked to tender for them, although, in the end, it was English Electric that tried manufacturing them, with a light alloy flange. The same light alloy was used for a set of experimental return rollers; however, on a Centurion test rig, they failed at a mere 18 miles. Initially, the road wheels were to have rubber rims, but on another test rig, these rubber components failed at 200 miles. Another set was tried after a redesign, and they failed at 350 miles. These results caused the designers to conclude that the tank was too heavy for rubber. This choice would have quite beneficial results later on when, during testing of the Conqueror's running gear, it was found impossible to cause the tank to shed its tracks. These tests were carried out in 1954, when the trials staff put the Conqueror through a series of manoeuvres in varied terrain and conditions. These conditions would have caused a Centurion to shed its tracks. On the larger and heavier Conqueror, there was no effect. The explanations for this were twofold. First, under some circumstances, the guide horn, which is the part of the track that fits inside the road wheels, would press onto the steel inside of the wheels. During the circumstances replicated during the trial, the guide horn would push against the rubber of the road wheel, which would then flex, allowing the guide horns to pass, resulting in a thrown track. The other suggestion for the better performance from the Conqueror was that the metal rims of the wheels would cut through debris such as mud, and maintain easier contact with the track surface. In comparison, the rubber rims on a Centurion just rode over the obstruction, again resulting in a thrown track. The trials also found that the loading on the guide horns was some 5 tons less than the Centurion. Even so, the trial did show that the Conqueror's tracks had very weak guide horns that needed strengthening.

In the late 1940s, at an early stage of the FV200's development, it was desired that the tank be genuinely 'universal'. Two strong requirements were for the vehicle to have the ability to be converted into a DD amphibian or be equipped with flame-throwing equipment as needed. One point that would generate a lot of contention over the following years was the fitting of a power take-off between the engine clutch and the gearbox. This change added an extra 7in to the length of the tank. The power take-off could be fitted with either a 7.5kW generator or a hydraulic pump.

These attachments would allow any FV200 to be equipped with a range of devices such as a flail or a dozer blade. Power for these accessory devices would be provided by multi-socket plugs dotted around the tank and tied directly into the primary electrical system. Controls for these sockets were located in the driver's compartment, allowing the driver to switch individual plugs and devices on or off at will. About 5 per cent of the tanks would be fitted with a dozer blade, which could be moved to its travelling position over the rear deck of the hull by linking the tracks to an attachment on the dozer blade assembly, then driving the tank in reverse.

The turret of the FV200 is a bit of a mystery that we will come to later on, but initially the armament was never in doubt. The vast majority of the tanks, about 90 per cent, were to be armed with a 20-pounder gun. The remaining 10 per cent were to be armed with a 95mm close-support howitzer; this was the same weapon that had been designed from a length of 3.7in anti-aircraft barrel and a 25-pounder breech during the Second World War and had served in various close-support tanks during the final two years of the conflict.

In October 1948 a review of firepower for the FV201 was carried out, and a desire for better anti-tank weapons was considered. The suggestion under discussion was to issue a single up-gunned FV201 per troop. The bigger gun was to be the 4.5in gun under development at the time. This weapon started life sometime in 1945 when the two boards dealing with weapon development were asked to design a weapon larger than a 20-pounder for use in the self-propelled anti-tank version of the A.45, which in turn would become the FV205. A trial was carried out using a 3.7in Mk 6 anti-aircraft gun to assess if loading inside a vehicle of the weapon of that size was even possible. The test found that it was possible to load such a long round, although loading would be easier if the round was shorter. Thus, the Chief Engineer of Artillery Design (CEAD) was asked to consider a gun that had a total length of 42in for the entire fixed round, and a maximum weight of 64lb.

The CEAD came up with a 4.5in high-velocity gun that fired an APDS (Armour-Piercing Discarding Sabot) projectile, with the total loaded weight of 24lb and the sub-projectile weighing 18lb. The shot had a muzzle velocity of some 4,000fps. The calculated armour penetration against 30-degree sloped armour was 326mm at zero yards, 298mm at 1,000 yards, and 271mm at 2,000 yards. The Secretary to the Artillery Board (SAB) reviewed the figures and disagreed with the CEAD's numbers. He suggested that same calibre gun with the same shell dimensions could have a 20lb APDS projectile, with a sub-projectile weighing 14lb. The muzzle velocity was increased to about 4,275fps. This shot, it was estimated, would, against a 30-degree slope, defeat 329mm at zero yards, 302mm at 1,000 yards, and 277mm at 2,000 yards. The two men were unable to agree, arguing back and forth. The main difference between the two was that the SAB version needed slightly more twist to its rifling to maintain accuracy. The main bone of contention was that the CEAD's version was better against skirts, spaced armour and obstructions, while the SAB's version saved in metals used to construct the sub-projectile, most noticeably tungsten carbide. Both men were summoned before the Ordnance Board after six months of complex mathematical arguments flying back and forth in memoranda. There the CEAD led off with his case and implied that there was some question about the accuracy of the SAB's design. The SAB retorted that the CEAD's advantage against skirts was a mere 1mm. Eventually, the board ruled that both solutions were viable; however, the economy in tungsten carbide was not a concern at present and the accuracy advantage was considered preferable, thus the recommendation to adopt the CEAD's solution was made.

This gun reappeared about eight months later when a set of armour criteria was given, and both the CEAD and SAB were asked if either solution could defeat the target. This new target was 152mm at 60 degrees and 2,000 yards, due to a reassessment of likely Soviet armour on the best-protected part of the tank; a secondary value of 80mm at 60 degrees, with 10mm skirts at 36in from the armour. The response from both the CEAD and SAB was akin to 'not a chance, even at point blank!'

When this gun was suggested for the FV201 the idea was killed off pretty quickly by the answer that there was still development potential in the 20-pounder that would likely beat the 4.5in performance, and the upcoming 20-pounder APDS Mk2 was about to start development, and so the idea of a bigger gun was dropped for now.

Very little has been said about the turret, and that is because the turret is one of the biggest enigmas of the entire project. Often, the documents mention a temporary Centurion turret being used. The problem with the turret is that while the plans available have a turret, they look awfully like the Centurion turret, although the back is slightly more sloped from the top view. At the time the plans were drawn in 1947, there was a plan to produce an improved Centurion turret for both the Centurion and FV200, and then design the fully-equipped FV200 turret.

The turrets shown on the plans certainly do not match with the textual description from other documents and are missing some critical features. One example, which is possibly the most glaring, is the range-finder, which would have added a bulge on the top of the Centurion turret raising the cupola by 4in. These plans are official documents, yet they still contain errors. For example, the transport diagram of the FV201 fitted with a flame-thrower includes the remote-control machine gun, which as we will see later should not have been mounted on such a set-up. At the time of writing, no one has found a dedicated turret schematic. This missing plan might be because the turret design was to have been finalized after all the hull components were finished, although there is one possible clue. Shortly after the FV200 project was abandoned, the requirements were handed to a class at the School of Tank Technology. The school is where British army officers were taught about how to design tanks, and over the years they have produced a great number of designs that were never going to be built. Most classes were given a problem, then told to design a tank to answer the requirements. In this case, the course was given the requirements of the now-cancelled FV200. The theoretical tank the students came up with, named 'Design Exercise Conqueror', was close to the FV200 as we know it, but with minor changes.

For example, the remote-control machine-gun turret was a different shape and mounted in the centre of the hull, not on the left over the tracks as was the case in the FV200. To add to the confusion, in this study, the students designed three different turret shapes. One of the turrets from this project may give us a clue to the FV200 turret, or it might be utterly misleading. For the artwork in this book, the existing drawings have been used; they are the official transport documents with the Centurion-style turret, even though these were all drawn before the hull was finalized and therefore before a turret was designed.

While the shape of the turret is unknown at the time of writing, its equipment is not. The turret was meant to be a thing of wonder in the post-war age. It would fit a 20-pounder gun which would be fully stabilized. To maintain the armour integrity, the gunner's primary sight was a reflector-cum-periscope (RCP). The gun had a device that would issue an audible tone over the intercom circuit to warn that it was off safe and ready to fire. This safety feature was removed after concerns about it interfering with fire commands. The turret also contained a range computer and a range-finder. The question was asked, in June 1948, if once the range was taken and the range computer calculated the holdover, could the gun be automatically laid to that range? The answer was yes, but consideration was needed for the gun moving on its own and if it would affect safety.

The commander was to be given an independent range-finder and RCP as well. Then the problems set in. First, the commander's range-finder would have to rotate with his cupola and, as range-finders need to be as wide as possible for accuracy, this would involve a considerable mass moving about on the top of the turret. The other problem was which form of range-finder was the best to use, stereoscopic or coincidence? A series of trials was carried out to find the best answer. The army sensibly enlisted the help of the navy, which had quite some experience with range-finders but these had never been used against armour. The tests were carried out using a Navy Mk 63 stereoscopic range-finder with a 1.8m base. During the trials, 90 per cent of test subjects were able to locate and range in on a tank. From this point of view, the test concluded, there would be no problems. A month later, another range-finder issue cropped up. The field of view from the proposed device was too small, by just 1 degree; 4 against the minimum requirement of 5 degrees. The lack of range-finders on the plans mentioned earlier is one of the discrepancies in the design of the turrets, which points towards the drawn turrets not being the actual FV200 versions.

With the advent of a fully-stabilized main gun, questions were raised about the rate of fire, and if the stabilization would interfere with the loading rate. To that end, in September 1946, a two-week trial was held to determine if this was the case. In this and a later trial, the times given are from when the loader starts to move to the moment he arms the gun's safety switch. Once again, a Centurion was modified; in this case, it was the third prototype of the A.41. The tank, by this time, had developed a steering fault and could only turn to the right. This mechanical failure was considered unimportant though. The tank had no stabilizer of its own, so the trial was limited to horizontal stabilization, which was simulated by the method of rotating the turret at the correct rate counter to the direction of turning. The main gun was locked to 2 degrees elevation.

The interior of the tank was modified with a rotating floor, but later the trials were repeated with a fixed floor. The gun itself was a 17-pounder, into which a dummy 20-pounder shell was loaded. The dummy shells had been manufactured by lathing down a lump of metal to the correct dimension, each weighing 47lb. As a 20-pounder-sized round will not fit into a 17-pounder breech no matter how hard you ram it, the rounds were loaded only up to the neck of the case, and a time penalty of one second applied. The latter was done so that the loading time could be compared to other tanks.

The movements of the two loaders used in the trial – one an experienced loader, the other a driver who was standing in for a loader – were filmed by two cameras. One camera was placed outside the tank and pointed through the shell ejection hatch. The other was set in the front hull of the tank facing backwards to film the loader's feet and movements when extracting rounds from bins in the side of the tank. Both loaders' times were combined to gain an average time, and then the mean time was taken from all the trials. One problem that was encountered was that the inexperienced loader, throughout the trial, became experienced and thus his times improved. As it turned out, the final time of 3.8 seconds under the best conditions was within less than a second of the 'real' times.

About the middle of 1947, another study of ammunition-handling was initiated. This time, a wooden mock-up of the tank's fighting compartment, including a 20-pounder, was constructed. For determining the rate of fire on the move, a Centurion Mk II was used and the difference between loading at the halt and on the move was calculated as a 50 per cent increase and applied to the times taken from the FV201 mock-up.

The turret layout had the commander and gunner located on the right of the turret turntable, with the commander at the rear of the turret. The loader was on the left of the gun, which cut the turret in two. In front of the loader was an ammunition bin containing nine rounds stored base-down. This rack was unarmoured on all sides. Under the gun was another bin, holding five rounds lying flat in line with the gun, which had armour on its right side, and the rounds could only be reached through the space occupied by the shells in the first rack. These fourteen rounds made up the tank's ready ammunition.

It might be useful at this point to explain the difference between ammunition classifications used by the British. A ready round is one that the loader can reach at any turret bearing, while the fighting rounds

The three-quarter view of the FV200 prototype, again showing off the distinctive machine-gun blister.

are ones that can be reached by the loader, but only when the turret is pointed in certain directions. Even if the blind spot where the round is unavailable is only a few degrees, it would still be considered a fighting round. The final group of rounds are replenishment rounds that cannot be reached, or cannot be reached safely, by the loader at any turret bearing. Replenishment rounds are used during lulls in combat to reload the fighting or ready racks within a tank. Usually, this required the crew to manhandle the rounds outside the tank.

Just five rounds were considered replenishment rounds, stored in the driver's compartment, of which three were stored vertically between the driver and hull gunner and two horizontally below the machine-gun blister. All the rest of the tank's total load of seventy-four rounds were classified as fighting rounds, and they were located in armoured bins along the side of the hull, and one three-round bin on the firewall between the fighting and engine compartment.

The trials on the mock-up also generated some suggestions for the production vehicle. First, a 1in toe board was requested to be fitted to the turret floor. The question of whether it would prove a hindrance to reaching for shells in the side bins was simply answered by the loading footage that showed the loaders cleared the lip of the turret floor by several inches and so the toe board would not impact on the loading in any way.

The other problem was that, as the stabilization would automatically traverse the turret if the loader was reaching for ammunition in the side bins, his hands and the shell would be outside of the turret basket. If the stabilizer turned the turret at the wrong moment, then it would lead to the loader's arms and the shell he was holding being crunched in the workings of the turret. The second modification that was suggested was a solution to this issue. The maximum speed of the rotation of the turret was worked out; from this the safety arc was determined and proposed to be marked on the floor. The safety arc showed the area in which ammunition could be taken from the side bins in safety with no danger from the turret turning and catching the loader's arms and the shell case.

The loader's position itself was considered remarkably free of projections and snags with one critical exception: his periscope was located exactly where his head would be while loading. The report suggests that the periscope should be moved forward; however, at this early stage in development, the 2in smoke bomb-thrower was in that position. The suggestion of multi-shot externally-mounted smoke dischargers was to be investigated if these proved viable, and then the periscope would be moved.

The turret design also caused some other issues for the designers at the time. The coaxial machine gun was to be a .30 calibre Browning; however, unlike on any previous tank, it was to be mounted further back and with heavier armour than had previously been used on a tank. The result would be that the barrel of the .30 Browning would be shrouded in armour for nearly all its length. This arrangement caused some worries about the air flow and thus the cooling of the barrel, considering the air flow was all but eliminated. If the gun was to overheat it would reduce barrel life dramatically, which would, in turn, mean a massive drop in accuracy over a prolonged engagement. The General Staff specifications called for the Browning to fire 100 rounds per minute for thirty minutes. This requirement was meant to simulate use in a battle where the tank would be shooting short bursts at targets over an extended period. To test this, a Sherman tank was wheeled out and used as a comparison. As this was in January 1947, no FV200 turret was available, so as usual in these tests, a Centurion was brought forth and modified to resemble the FV200. In this case, a Centurion Mk I had armour mounted over its machine gun, and the gun switched to a Browning. A specially-constructed thermocouple was used to take the measurements during the tests; however, after 7.5 minutes of 100 rounds per minute, as the Sherman's Browning passed a barrel temperature of 520 degrees Centigrade, this instrument broke and a standard one had to be used for follow-up tests. Not that this test needed to be repeated. The temperatures were close to the same in the FV200-style mount, with no more than 10 degrees of difference. At the rate of 100 rounds per minute, the Browning in the FV200 failed after about fifteen minutes. A lower rate of fire of sixty-seven rounds per minute was tried, and the FV200 managed that. So another test was carried out using eighty rounds per minute, and again both guns passed that test. To check their numbers were correct, an M191A5 air-cooled tripod-mounted gun was fired in the same test criteria. It too seemed to confirm the magic number of about 695-700 degrees was the point at which the Browning's barrel began to be inaccurate. In summary, the report pointed out that no mount with the .30 calibre Browning would reach the desired rate of fire. At the same time as the rate of fire test, measurements of the carbon dioxide build-up were taken at positions throughout the tank. It was found that basic Centurion Mk I levels of ventilation would keep the crew safe.

Chapter 3

Universal Engineering

In June and August of 1945, the Fighting Vehicles Design Establishment began discussing with the Royal Engineers precisely what they required in a tank. This conversation resulted in two versions of the A.45 being modified into Armoured Vehicle Royal Engineers (AVRE) tanks. The first was the AVRE(T), with the 'T' standing for 'turret'. This version would be a normal A.45 with a demolition gun. Two guns were considered for the role of demolition gun on the AVRE(T). Although both guns had similar performance, with a muzzle velocity of 850fps and a chamber pressure of just under 2 tons per square inch, they were very different weapons. The larger of the two was a 7.5in weapon designed by Major Jefferis of the famous MD1, and in some documents was called the Jefferis gun, which is not to be confused with the identically-named PIAT prototype. This weapon was utterly conventional, with a vertical sliding breech block and automatic case ejection. The breech mechanism failed on the first round of test firing. After such a poor start, the gun was stripped and oiled and then began to function correctly. However, it was found that the gun was extremely violent when it recoiled, which caused some concern to the crew.

The second weapon was of a smaller 6.5in calibre, and it was somewhat different to a normal gun. It was designed by Sir Charles Dennistoun Burney, who is also associated with the 'Burney gun' infantry anti-tank weapon. It featured a 45-degree sliding breech block, but the loader did not have to worry about the case. The entire round was a single piece, with the charge in the rear part of the projectile. There were several large holes in the base of the projectile sealed with brass or copper foil. When the charge was electrically fired, the foil would be disintegrated, allowing the gasses to propel the round out of the barrel, leaving no case behind. This method of disposing of the case with the shell was seen as a big advantage over the 7.5in weapon. The complete

6.5in shell was a heavier round, but its longer length made it easier to handle than the abnormally short 7.5in round. The two guns were fitted to a Churchill AVRE in 1947 for comparative trials. The General Staff specification called for 100 per cent of rounds to hit a 3ft square target at 200 yards, and 50 per cent to hit a 6ft square target at 400 yards. Both guns achieved this requirement with ease. However, just after the start of the trials, the 7.5in weapon was rejected by the War Office with approval from the Ministry of Supply. This decision, on the face of it, seems odd. Why conduct trials if you are going to select a weapon halfway through before the trials have reported?

On top of that, the 6.5in weapon, manufactured by William Beardmore's, for whom Burney had worked and filled patents on Burney's work, was of diabolically bad build quality. Not one part of the weapon functioned anywhere near as desired. Parts were missing or poorly fitted. The extent of this was apparent when nearly every single piece of the gun's operation had to be modified during the trial. The gun also had, sometimes, a quite horrifying level of flashback, even in weather conditions that were not conducive to causing this effect. The flashback, although alarming, was found to be short-lived and considered insufficient to cause any charring. However, trials a year later started

Two pictures demonstrating loading inside an FV3903 AVRE. It is immediately clear why the unique shell design had a handle fitted on its base. Once the shell is ready to be loaded and in a more convenient position, the handle would be unscrewed and discarded before the gun is loaded.

off firing a shell that had been left over from the previous trials. This round caused significant flashback that charred the loader's beret and left shards of imperfectly disintegrated hot foil in the breech.

There was a method to the War Office's decision. The trials had initially been scheduled to be held during February 1946, allowing for time to review the trial results. These had been unavoidably delayed, and the decision on which gun to use needed to be made without delay.

Above, left and opposite: Before and after photographs showing the destructive power of the 6.5in BL gun. The first target is a trio of oil drums, filled with reinforced concrete; the location where they were sited is shown in the second picture. One round from the 6.5in gun has utterly destroyed them. A similar story has happened with the large concrete slab in the second series of pictures. One round and it is reduced to rubble.

Therefore, in 1947 just after the start of the trials, the government chose the 6.5in gun, possibly because it would allow for a greater amount of ammunition to be carried within the tank.

It may be that the government regretted this choice when, in 1951, the United States decided to purchase several hundred of the 6.5in BL Mk I

25

gun for their use. As news of this broke, William Beardmore's contacted the government demanding a large sum of royalties for the fifteen patents included in the gun. The government refuted this, admitting that two of the patents were applicable, but the other thirteen had not been used. This disagreement created a file about 1.5in thick in the archives, with both sides' lawyers arguing with each other. Despite this, the AVRE(T) was to be armed with the 6.5in weapon.

Both the AVRE versions were also able to carry assault bridges or mount the Canadian Indestructible Roller Device (CIRD) for mine-clearing.

The AVRE(L) was a completely different idea. The 'L' stands for 'launcher', and it was to be an armoured box with a set of ramps on either end and a trackway across the roof, much like the Churchill ARK in concept. These ramps were about 15ft in length and, when laid, giving a total length of 71ft. Some documents suggest that the ramps were linked to rams using a cordite charge to launch them into position as fast as possible. In addition, the AVRE(L) could carry fascines or a 50/60-ton raft on its roof. The roof also had two roof hatches that were 1.5ft wide and 2ft long. These, along with a pair of side doors, which according to the specifications had to be the equivalent size of those on a Churchill, were to allow the twelve passengers to be able to disembark. These were intended to be demolition parties and to carry out other engineering tasks. The crew was set at three as well as the passengers: a commander, driver and hull gunner whose job it was to man the single hull machine gun.

The AVRE(L) was also seen as the basis for a future load carrier and FV212 heavy armoured personnel carrier.

Models for both designs were available in the final three months of 1945 and, by January 1946, a full-size mock-up made of 1in mild steel was under construction, which was scheduled to be dispatched to the Experimental Bridging Establishment at Christchurch for evaluation.

While mentioning the AVREs and their attachments, a number of trials and studies were carried out in 1946. These were to work out what was needed for the flail specifications and an improvement to the CIRD mine rollers. The flail was to be fittable to any A.45, while the CIRD was only for AVREs.

The mathematical study that went into the flail started by calculating the minimum beat pattern needed. This was achieved by working out the smallest possible triangle into which the smallest contemporary anti-tank

This is the FV222, the Armoured Recovery Vehicle based on the Conqueror hull. The general arrangement of the superstructure is very similar to the FV203 AVRE(L), although the ramps and the hatch arrangements are missing.

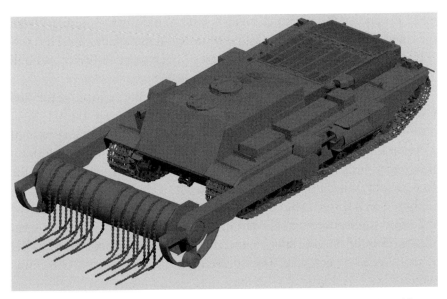

Artist's impression of the FV216 independent flail unit. Although designed it was never built, but a competitor in the shape of the Churchill Toad was constructed and still exists today, fully restored and in working order.

mine could fit (anti-personnel mines were not to be considered). From there, calculations showed how to ensure that the flails beat each corner of the triangle as the tank advanced. As with most things in armour design, there were a great many factors to consider and they forced the design to a conclusion. For example, the highest possible speed of the tank is desired to cross a stretch of ground, but to do so, many more chain flails per rotator would be needed, which in turn radically drives up the weight and thus the horsepower requirements to drive the rotator. Equally, the study showed that if there were more than twelve rows of flails fitted, a mine detonated by one set of flails would damage the following set of chains with its explosion as they would be closer to the mine than the preceding set. At the other end of the scale, less than six rows of flails would mean the rotator torque became unbalanced. The net result was that the flail would need to impact the ground at a rate of eighty-four times per foot of advance. If the flail was rotating at 145rpm, then the tank could advance at just over 1mph. Increasing the rotator speed towards the theoretical maximum of 180rpm would allow the tank to progress faster.

The doctrine on the use of flails was to have troops of four. These would 'flog' with two tanks forward, with a gap less than the width of the flail between them. The second pair would be to the rear but offset and overlapping the two forward tanks, which would create a lane through the minefield that was 24 to 30ft wide, or about the width of three tanks.

The improvement studied for the CIRD mine rollers was the attachment of a vibration unit. Some civilian users had reported their findings of using vibrations during soil compaction. Someone in the War Office then suggested attaching the vibration devices to the CIRD to save weight. The idea was that the vibrations increased the downward force, thus simulating additional weight of the device and so triggering the mine's fuse. If the vibrators worked as the calculations suggested they would and increased downward force, then the rollers could be lighter, which in turn would mean less horsepower needed to drive the rollers, and a smaller, lighter engine. The design called for two contra-rotating out-of-balance weighted disks located above the mine roller, with their axis of spin 90 degrees from that of the rollers in the horizontal plane. It was found that this arrangement would indeed save weight and horsepower. While using the CIRD, the tank's speed would be limited to 5mph. A 1/4th scale model of the CIRD was built, but its results were found to be inconsistent.

This Churchill AVRE has been equipped with the CIRD. The vibration units were proposed to be fitted on the arms with the rollers. Their exact location was on the end of the arms directly above the rollers.

The other requirement that appeared in 1947 was for an FV200 bridge-layer that could span a 45ft gap. A Centurion had its body made up to the same width as an FV200, and a 54ft bridge was fixed to the top. The experiments even considered whether the hump of the bridge should be pointing up or down. The mock-up was driven around the roads surrounding Chobham in Surrey. These quiet little English villages posed no difficulties, although the report does point out that no tight corners were encountered.

The set-up was also trialled on a cross-country course, and it was found that the hump-down arrangement improved off-road performance due to the extreme points of the bridge having higher ground clearance. It was found that the vehicle commander was vital to the vehicle manoeuvring in close country.

The No.1 FV200 prototype was mechanically very different to the No.2, which was the same standard as the production vehicle was

The Centurion modified to resemble the FV208 bridge-layer. The width of the two tanks can be compared by the skirts being held away from the hull to represent the wider FV200 series hull.

In this picture, the mock-up is demonstrating why 'hump down' is better for cross-country travel.

destined to be. The No.2 tank was also to be completed as a DD tank to test the equipment. Later in 1947, the decision to place a Centurion Mk III turret armed with a 17-pounder on the No.2 prototype would be taken. At first, in 1945, floats for the DD role were considered, but these would be too large and vulnerable to enemy fire. As pontoons were rejected, the only other option open to the designers was the fitting of a screen much like the Sherman DD tanks of the Second World War. At the same time, propulsion was considered. At first, an outboard motor was suggested, although track propulsion was also looked at. To achieve the required 6kn, grousers would have had to be fitted to the tracks, which would have knock-on effects once the tank had landed. When the screen was erected, the gun was stowed to the rear.

Later in the development of the FV200, the DD requirement would cause even more anguish among the designers. The overhang at the rear of the tank was 2.5ft. When the naval architects saw this, they worried that, when being launched from the ramp of a landing craft, the overhang at the rear of the tank would hit the ramp, pitching the tank forward. In doing so, the front part of the DD screen would reach below the water line and the tank would founder. The suggested solution was to give the DD screen a canvas roof, which would solve the problem and would provide the DD tank with better seakeeping.

The power take-off would be linked to propellers, and a rudder would be provided. However, the take-off did not provide sufficient horsepower to achieve the speed required, so a reduced speed of 5.8kn was accepted. The DD screen was to be stored in an armoured box the designers called a Topee that ran around the top of the hull. This container was to prevent damage to the screen so it could be re-used at will. This box would also cause many problems during development. First, someone spotted a possible foul for turret traverse at the 6 o'clock position along with a limit to the driver's visibility. To test the impact of the latter, a Centurion was modified to simulate the Topee. The other worry was the gun depression being interfered with by the screen container.

Angle of Traverse	Degree of Depression
	With Topee
0	10 (full depression)
10	10
20	8
30	4.5
40	2.75
90	3

As can be seen, the screen sliced off a fraction of the depression, culminating at 2.5 degrees less depression at 90 degrees traverse. The main concern was that this would compromise the gun stabilizer. At the RAC conference in 1947, three options to solve this dilemma were presented and discussed. The first was to continue on course and accept the loss of depression and the reduction in the fighting ability of the tank. The next was to fold the screen outwards. However, this would make the tank much wider, up to 15ft 4in. The final option was to have the screen as single use and jettison it after landing. At the conference, the unanimous vote was for the third option.

The fighting ability of the DD tank was also considered when at sea. It was recognized that, during the run-in, over the last 500 yards DD tanks were open to attack, and so the idea of mounting remote-control machine guns on the screen was suggested. These did not need sighting and would carry 1,500 rounds in one continuous belt per gun, giving three to five minutes of fire. A high portion of the belt was to be tracer, and the commander would be controlling the gun and using the tracer to guide the suppressive fire. The two guns were to either be on a single mount on the bow, with both guns mounted coaxially, or on two mountings with the guns linked together but mounted separately, and having a convergence set to 1,000 yards. Either mount was to have an elevation and depression of 30 degrees. Although a General Staff requirement was raised for this system, no inventor seems to have felt like having an attempt at solving the problem.

There was also talk of making the FV208 bridge-layer amphibious. It was considered easier to float the bridge and the tank separately, but was preferred to have the tank floated with the bridge in place.

Chapter 4

Flame in the Dark

From the outset, the requirement for a universal tank included a flame-throwing capacity that could be installed on any tank, in the field, in just six hours. To that end, every FV201 was to be fitted with the pipework and electric wiring required for flame-throwing. This equipment consisted of a pipe running from the rear plate, the length of the hull and up to a hole in the roof plate. The hole was covered when not in use, and when converted to flame the covering plate was used to cover the gap caused by the removal of the machine-gun blister. The other alteration was a towing bar fitted to the back of the tank, as the rear wall was not strong enough to be used to haul the loaded trailer.

With the firm requirement for flame-throwing, work began almost at the start of the life of the A.45. In November 1946 the first query about the equipment was raised: where would the weapon be mounted? The controller would be the hull gunner. The suggestions included replacing the machine gun in its blister with the flame-thrower, construction of a new blister on the opposite side of the hull, replacing the original machine-gun blister with a rotatable sub-turret or even stacking the flame-thrower blister on top of the existing one. All of these options had limitations, the most common being a limited arc to one side, and failing to meet the fairly wide-angle requirements of 120 degrees either side of the centreline; many added weight or required significant redesign of the roof plate. Two positions on the turret were considered: these were dead centre beside the commander's hatch and in a blister on the left side of the turret. As well as restricted arc there were added complications in the controls and fuel feed, both of which would need to be routed into the turret, which would require its rotation maintained. Eventually, the location of the centre of the glacis low down was selected as it had the least number of negatives associated with it. These were that it limited the driver's vision in that direction, and the fuel had to be brought to the flame-thrower. Two options for this were to either cut a hole in the glacis plate or route the pipe through the roof

Above and below: Artist's impression of the FV201 fitted with a Red Cyclops. For the trailer the only plans available to work with were a single cross-section, so the actual shape along the sides might be different.

plate and down the front of the glacis. Cutting a hole in the frontal armour would seriously compromise the FV201's protection, so the latter choice was taken. A fully armoured shroud around the pipe was built into the fabric of the tank, dead centre of the glacis, and is shown on plans.

With the location decided, work began on the design and construction of the flame gun. The design had two settings that allowed different fuel flow rates. When it was built, the first flame gun was too long and at certain elevations it fouled the tank's 20-pounder. To avoid this, the distance

34

between the crown of the projector and the centre of the gun had to be reduced; the only way to do this was to remove the dual flow equipment. This fixed-flow rate was accepted in the short term; however, the requirement of the variable flow rate between 4 to 10 gallons per second was maintained as a long-term specification.

While this was going on, in April 1947 a trial was carried out with a Sherman DD towing a Crocodile trailer. The aim was to see if a trailer could be used on a DD tank fitted for flame, as there were a lot of bad points about having the fuel inside the tank such as the removal of large amounts of main gun ammunition and the obvious safety concerns. So far no copy of the report can be found, but it seems that the Crocodile trailer had some leakage problems and the suggestion to the army was a flotation tank, which was received with resignation but acceptance along with the proposal that the flotation tanks be jettisonable, or the use of a sealant compound such as Bostik, which was immediately jumped on by the army officers who suggested that the engineers should be able to create a watertight seal with welding.

In mid-1947 the current proposal of the army's flame-thrower equipment received its Rainbow code-name. This was a way of naming equipment without giving away its purpose to any potential Soviet spies. A colour was chosen along with a random word to name the items. For example, Green Mace was the Rainbow code for a 5in water-cooled AA

A photograph taken during the trials with the Sherman DD towing the Crocodile trailer. Here the DD tank is in the water and has successfully been launched, with the trailer following it down the ramp. Lashed to the top of the trailer was a large inflated ring to give buoyancy.

gun with a rate of fire of ninety-six rounds per minute, or Blue Peacock which was the British army's chicken-warmed nuclear demolition mine. Several aircraft radars also used the code colour Blue, and when in later years Blackburn Buccaneers were delivered without their Blue Parrot radars fitted but with lumps of concrete in their place to simulate the weight, it gave rise to jokes about 'Blue Circle radar'.

The idea of the colour not being related to the function of the equipment failed a bit when flame-throwing equipment was issued the code colour Red, the flame equipment for FV201 being Red Cyclops, and the flame trailer receiving the number FV3701. The flame-thrower requirements were for a 400-gallon trailer, with the need for variable flow rate reintroduced, the minimum effective range to be 200 yards. To achieve this performance the 'muzzle velocity' of the flame gun was 220fps and the operating pressure 500psi. The arc of fire was to be a huge 120 degrees each side of the centre line; of that, 75 degrees were to be at full gun depression. As the hull gunner would be using the machine gun's sight, there would be considerable blind spots that he could not see. This flaw was anticipated, and the idea of the commander aiming the shots by giving fire commands was adopted; for this purpose, the gunner was given a dial to indicate the flame gun's bearing. Once again, concerns about the DD tanks' Topee raised their head, with the box blocking the flame gun and limiting its traverse and depression. There was a tentative suggestion to raise the flame gun's pedestal. However, that would likely have interfered with the main gun depression. In the end, the aforementioned decision to make the DD screen jettisonable solved the question.

The Red Cyclops trailer was similar to the Crocodile, having a pair of the same 18in tyres. There were four versions of the armour layout on the trailer initially. These ranged from a version with 8mm of armour on all surfaces, which was judged to be proof from shell bursts from a 25-pounder at over 40ft, to the most heavily armoured version with 14mm everywhere. The latter was judged to be proof against point-blank small-arms fire and 25-pounder shells at 5ft. The third option was a 10mm plate, which would give shrapnel protection only. Weights ranged from 13 tons down to 11.72 tons depending on the armour levels. The final design selected was the fourth armour scheme which comprised parts of all these designs. On upper surfaces, they had the 10mm protection to protect against shell bursts, but judged that small-arms protection on the roof of the trailer was wasted. The sides, however, would be exposed to the full force of the enemy's small arms so received the full 14mm protection. Finally, plates on the underside that were very unlikely to be hit were listed as 8mm to save weight. The final weight was 12.53 tons.

About the same time, in July 1947, concerns were raised about how much spare manpower in research departments was available for work on Red Cyclops, which meant that it was impractical to get the flame-thrower development under way before 1949. In turn, this would result in an in-service date of 1953, two years after the FV201 was predicted to be in service.

The manpower issue appeared again on 7 October 1948, only this time concerning the production cost. A report was filed on this date on Red Cyclops that caused some concern. Early in 1947, a civil servant had been tasked with finding out the costs of Red Cyclops. However, the design was too immature to be costed until later in 1948. When the report landed, it had some uncomfortable information. The report compared Red Cyclops to the Second World War Crocodile. The latter had cost just £2,000 per unit and taken about 3,250 man hours to produce. Red Cyclops in comparison was looking at a likely cost of about £11,500 and 17,450 man hours per unit. In reality, this was a conservative estimate; the two Red Cyclops prototype units that were built cost more than £15,000 each. The breakdown of costs gives us some idea of how Red Cyclops was arranged. Inside the trailer were ten 11in-bore fuel cylinders, each containing 40 gallons of 'Red Vulcan', the thickened fuel that was required to achieve the required range. At the top of each of these cylinders was a piston driven by a 4lb cordite charge. At the bottom, these cylinders were linked to a 46-gallon accumulator. When the cordite charge was fired, it forced the piston down which filled the accumulator. The empty cylinder was then filled with 2,000psi air, which in turn kept the accumulator at 500-600psi. When the gunner fired, it opened a valve on the accumulator which drove the rest of the fuel system. When the accumulator reached 4 gallons, the system automatically fired another charge and repeated the process. The reason for such a severe method of handling the fuel was due to the extreme viscosity of Red Vulcan.

The trailer also contained a heating system to keep the fuel at 37.7 degrees C. Trials had shown that heating the fuel achieved a significant range increase: with unheated fuel the range had been a mere 120 yards; with heated, the range had jumped up to 300 yards.

Inside the tank, seventeen rounds of main gun ammunition had been removed and a compressor fitted; this fed to the flame gun that used electrical spark ignition.

To achieve the performance listed earlier, thickened fuel needed to be used; this and the complicated wiring kit required to control the cylinder motors were the main contributors to the cost. A meeting was arranged in short order to see what could be done to the bill that was looming in front of the War Office. This meeting organized a working party to find ways of lowering the costs, and they came up with five options. First on the table was simplicity itself: take the Crocodile design and 'hot it up'. This option would work, but the thicker fuel would require higher pressures and thus an increase in weight of all the pipework and cylinders. Next came the idea of wiring the flame gun directly to two fuel cylinders. These, in turn, would connect to about forty 10lb cordite charges for propellant. When some of the propellant was used it would push 8 to 10 per cent of the fuel down the pipe and out of the gun; all the flame gun needed was an ignition source. Idea number three was to have low-pressure tanks constantly feeding into a line, resulting in a dotted line effect with 5-gallon blobs at half-second intervals. A variant on this system was the fourth solution. The main difference was fitting a turbine pump (a device used to start jet engines) or even a lightweight aircraft engine to give pressure to the fuel line. The fifth and final solution does not seem to have much in the way of details, just that it involved a pourable fuel called A.1 Butilate that had water injected into it between the storage tanks and the flame gun to create the desired thickened fuel. All of these would involve extra design time, most causing about eighteen months' delay; however, the fifth solution, it was estimated, would need another three years' work, if it was even possible.

With all these costs, some began to question the need for flame at all. To answer this, Mr E. Drake Seager was commissioned to create a report on the 'FV201 flame-thrower against the *Panzerfaust*'. It is an old saying that the army always fights the last war, and the choice of a German wielding a *Panzerfaust* seems an odd choice for an opponent at first glance. However, there does seem to be an element of sense to it. First, the army recognized that it is likely that any enemy they were to face would have a weapon of similar capabilities to the *Panzerfaust*, and the defensive abilities of the FV201 were not to be judged just by the effect of the flame-thrower on the type of defence. The effectiveness of the *Panzerfaust* can be gauged by the rise in British tank casualties during the North-West European campaign. In Normandy tanks knocked out by hollow-charge weapons amounted to just 10 per cent; by the end of the war that had risen to 35 per cent. This kill rate was aided by the Germans' tactics. They would site *Panzerfausts* to fire down fixed lanes of sight crossing the line of advance. As a tank advanced it would expose its side to first one, then subsequent *Panzerfaust* positions. This tactic would also limit the ability of the Allies to observe the location and drastically cut down the amount of fire they could use against the area.

The key measurement Mr Seager used to determine the effectiveness of the flame-thrower was the '90 per cent zone'. This area was similar to working out the grouping of a normal gun. It is merely the area into which 90 per cent of the fuel fired from the flame gun lands. The trouble was that at this time Mr Seager did not know the size of the 90 per cent zone, and so had to work out effectiveness for a number of zones; these ranged from 10 yards up to 50 yards, in 10-yard increments.

For baseline effectiveness Mr Seager used two sets of tests carried out in the Second World War. The first used an early mark of Wasp carrier; the

A close-up of the Crocodile flame gun, as fitted to the Centurion. Unlike the fit to a Churchill, the ignition coils are next to the nozzle of the flame-thrower.

second used a Crocodile. The main difference between the two was that the Crocodile equipment had a nozzle on its flame gun; this made quite a difference. Either system hitting a trench from the side would destroy the position. Tests were carried out up to 60-yard ranges. From the front, however, at 60 yards the Wasp required a wet shot before the ignited shot; this allowed the fuel to seep into the trench and increased the density of fuel on the ground. A Crocodile could achieve the same effect with a single hot shot from 60 yards. The Wasp was also used in a series of tests with it firing while moving at speeds ranging from 10 to 20mph. These were utterly ineffective if the people in the trench took the precaution of ducking.

Another trial involving a Crocodile had a series of slit trenches dug in an open field on the reserve slope of a hill. These were laid out in the standard German formation. The Crocodile then approached at 5mph with the commander's head out. Then the trial was tried again with the commander buttoned down. In both tests, the crew of the tank failed to spot the positions in time to effectively engage them, although in one trial the commander saw one trench in time to get orders to his crew to fire a snap shot that went high.

Even working with just this data, Mr Seager came up with the rather exact figure of needing 0.125 gallons of fuel per square yard to achieve casualties and thus would need eight, one-second shots into an area to destroy all the trenches in it. However, a lesser number of shots, about four, would sufficiently neutralize the area to allow the FV201 to pass, and should someone fire on the tank then the remaining shots could be fired. The army's doctrine was much more brutally simple. Two platoons would approach to within flame range of a hostile position, covered by the headquarters and two troops using their main guns. Then the forward troops would fire at an angle along the line. Such a deployment was designed to create the maximum saturation. Then the platoons would leapfrog down the enemy line, each flaming in turn.

The 'Panzerfaust' report helped fuel the argument for the flame-thrower on the FV201. By now it was January 1949, but the problem of how much Red Cyclops would cost was still seen as critical. One suggestion was removing the 200-yard minimum range requirement, while it was possible that feature could be dropped it was disliked quite heavily by both the Royal Armoured Corps and the infantry. The main concern was that a lower range would mean higher infantry casualties. Also, the increased stand-off and the likelihood of a better firing position with increased range were not overlooked. At the sixty-fourth meeting of the Weapon Development Committee the minutes listed the five previous solutions given to lower the cost of Red Cyclops and the projected savings. However, a sixth solution had been added. It was listed as using an entirely new principle and would be developed by an outside company which would avoid any delay. In a pencilled note on minutes, it was introduced as the FV3702, which subsequently received the Rainbow code of Red Hermes.

This new principle involved a pressure vessel of 22mm armour plate. Inside the pressure vessel was a bag which contained the fuel. An inert gas was fed into the pressure vessel, squeezing the bag and providing pressure to the fuel system. One advantage of this was that when the fuel was refilled it would return the inert gas into its cylinder so there should be no loss of gas that would need refilling.

This equipment was mounted on a two-wheeled armoured trailer, and a Rolls-Royce B.40 Mk IIA engine was fitted to provide pressure to the pump, although it was downrated to just 55hp. The pressure vessel would be supplied by Templewood Engineering Co. and the rest of the work by Rover Ltd. Rover was then informed that they would need to provide a full set of equipment for a comparative demonstration at the end of September that year. The display would involve the two pieces of Red Cyclops equipment that had been manufactured. Up until that point, the cost of the two Red Cyclops trailers was over £30,000, which if the General Staff requirement of 25 per cent of the FV201 fleet to have flame-throwing equipment was fitted would mean a cost of somewhere around £3,116,500. In comparison, Red Hermes would cost just £1,680,200 for the same number of units.

Rover was warned, clearly, that the budget for Red Hermes was tight and if costs began to rise too much the entire project would be cancelled. It seems that the Weapon Development Committee was willing to investigate Red Hermes, but should it prove too expensive or fail to work, then progress on Red Cyclops was sufficient for them to pick up from that point with almost no delay. For this reason, and because the development of Red Cyclops had provided significant technical advances, it was decided to complete the prototype stage but stop short of production. Rover said there was about two months' work once the final drawings were delivered. For the development of both systems, a Sherman would stand in during trials.

At roughly the same time the United States had been working on flame-throwers for their medium tanks. In the interests of standardization, it was decided that both countries' flame trailers would be interchangeable.

Although the flame gun itself would be different as the United States required their gunner to operate the flame gun, two types of gun were to be assessed and these were described as a 'spherical nozzle' or an 'Adder gun'-style weapon. The weapon was to be mounted on the forward left portion of the glacis. It would have a –20 degrees depression and a +30 degrees elevation, although +60 degrees was desired, and could slew through this at 18 degrees per second. By now (as we will shortly see), the FV201 had been cancelled and this equipment was to be fitted to a Centurion.

By this point, Red Hermes had been cancelled, and the flame-throwing equipment the British were looking at developing was adapting Crocodile equipment to be mounted on the glacis of a Centurion. At the end of 1951, the holdings of Crocodile trailers amounted to 29 operational and 391 that could be repaired. This flame-thrower equipment was also briefly considered for being fitted to the new medium tank under consideration. In the summer of 1952, the 30th Armoured Brigade (TA) was due to undergo training on the Centurion-Crocodile training. However, in the end, the usual problem that afflicts British weapon development – the lack of money – caused the requirement for flame-throwing to be dropped in April 1954.

The complete Centurion Crocodile. The large and bulky box mounting the flame gun would likely include several components for which there was no room inside the tank. On an FV200 these would have been incorporated during the design stage, hence the smaller size shown in the artwork earlier.

Chapter 5

Conquering Cancellation

There you have a rough idea of the technical aspects of the most advanced tank in the world at the time. So, what happened to it? Why did it not reach the soldiers at the front lines and why did the Centurion, despite its many flaws when compared to the FV201, continue in service?

In August 1946 a note was issued stating the number of FV200s required by the army. The production schedule was set at 240 tanks being needed, at a rate of twenty per month, for the financial year 1947/1948. Each of these tanks was budgeted to cost £20,000. However, this was on top of the 240 tanks that should have been in production in the 1946/1947 financial year. Even at the first step, at a time when the design of the tank had not yet been finished, production was a year behind. Two weeks later the realities of the situation had set in and the 1947/1948 production was written down to just 100, and even that was considered optimistic. If this plan was accepted, then the production rate in 1949/1950 would have to be forty per month. Even this hope was sunk at the very end of the month when the Ministry of Supply stated that it could not meet the twenty per month requirement.

By November a clue surfaces in the documents. The army was desperate for new tanks; however, the cost implications were causing problems. To give an idea of the scale of the problem, in October 1948 all light tanks were removed from the organization of the army. The FV300 series should have taken their place, but in desperation to save money the development pace of the FV300 was slowed and Cromwells with their turrets removed were to be used instead. To meet these financial constraints, the Centurion was to stand in as the new universal tank until the FV201 was developed.

In December there was the suggestion of the No.2 prototype being held up to fix the Topee problems detailed earlier. On the same day it was suggested, this idea was rejected.

Cost reared its head again in March 1947. The original aim for the fleet was to have 5 per cent of the tanks equipped with dozer blades. Although this remained the General Staff's commitment during wartime, the cost of producing those dozer attachments meant that the entire idea had to be dropped.

By October 1947, at a point when some 120 tanks were originally scheduled to be produced, the first prototype became operational. The AVRE(T) had finished being designed – a process that had started precisely two years earlier – and the AVRE(L) mock-up had been completed, the building of the mock-up having started at the same time as the design of the AVRE(T). Three months later in January 1947, English Electric was issued a contract to begin building the AVRE(T) prototype, using a Centurion turret Mk III in place of the undersigned FV200 one.

In October 1948 the FV212 heavy APC finally succumbed and the requirement was dropped. Two years earlier it had been stated as a firm

One of the FV200 prototypes, possibly No.3, with a Centurion turret being used for weighted running trials. The suggestion that it might be Prototype No.3 is from the weights added to the glacis in the location of the flame gun mount.

requirement due to the need to give infantry the same level of protection as tank crew; however, the AVRE(L) was to serve as the basis for the vehicle and that was so far behind schedule that it had left the FV212 in limbo for several years. Because of this, it was felt that the project had run its course and as we will see, the concept of the APC had shifted away from the heavy APC idea. The same month saw the first addition to the family since the original change to FV numbers. The FV213 Beach armoured recovery vehicle was listed as a requirement. On the plus side, the first trials report on the No.1 prototype tank was submitted.

October 1948 also marks a significant date: the birth of the Conqueror. As we have seen with the discussions on the 4.5in gun, there was a constant urge to increase the anti-tank ability of the FV200 series. There was a dilemma in choosing the gun: the 20-pounder and the United States' 90mm weapons could work as a main gun able to fire high-explosives at a sufficient rate of fire; these were termed 'supporting fire' weapons. However, they would be lacking in anti-tank performance. On the reverse, the 120mm guns could work as an anti-tank weapon, but would not have the rate of fire to work as 'supporting fire' weapons. One solution was to dust off the idea used for deploying the Firefly, giving each troop a tank that had the best anti-tank firepower. This firepower dilemma gave rise to two new classes of tank: the medium gun tank and the heavy gun tank. English can sometimes be a tricky language and those class designations can be and have been misread. To clarify the terminology, the weights given in the name refer not to the weight of the tank, but the size of the gun and its primary role. Heavy gun tanks were for killing enemy armour, and medium gun tanks were for general duty tank roles.

To this end, just five days after the conversation about fitting the 4.5in gun into the FV201, on 19 October a report was requested for improvements to the anti-tank firepower of the FV200. Alternative specifications for the proposed vehicle were requested, but some considerations were suggested. These included the best possible anti-tank performance while dropping the need for smoke and HE shells; a minimum of thirty rounds of ammunition, and the acceptance of two-piece ammunition. The specifications also included the option to allow a limited traverse tank and two standards of accuracy. The first and most hoped-for requirement was at the same level as the 20-pounder, although worsened accuracy was allowed as meeting the standards of the 75mm from a Sherman.

The bad news for the FV201 kept coming in 1949. The DD prototype's completion date had stretched from December 1949 to March 1950. The army kept plugging away with the DD work for two reasons. First, if they cancelled work on it the navy would halt their work on launching tanks from LCT Mk 8, meaning that it would not be until the navy started work on the LCT Mk 9 that the capability to launch tanks would be regained. LCT Mk 9 was a nebulous future craft on which the navy did not envisage starting work until the second year of any future major war. Equally, the army lacked any information or knowledge of DD tanks in this weight class, so they wanted to keep on working on it to gain experience.

In June things were beginning to become desperate, and a paper was called for with the sole aim of providing FV201s for troop trials, without delay.

With the situation spiralling out of control and under severe financial pressure, about five years after the project started and with only a handful of prototypes partially produced, the army had to decide what it was going to do. In July 1949 the situation came to a climax, and the way forward was thrashed out by heads of the army. On 12 July 1949, the report on improving the tank's firepower was submitted. This new tank was numbered the FV214. Weighing in at 60 tons, she was too heavy for DD equipment. This simplified things massively as the power take-off could be removed, shortening the tank and saving weight. These weight savings could be applied to armour protection. The glacis was sloped back even more than on the FV201 to 60 degrees. This meeting also gave birth to a new tank: the FV221. This vehicle was in response to the calls to get the chassis into troop trials with the utmost speed. The idea was that a small number of these tanks would be produced with Centurion turrets. This turret was to be a standard Centurion Mk III, although it was not to include any stabilization equipment. The FV221 would be identical in every way apart from the turret and the roof plate. This solution would provide experience with the running gear and the chassis of the tank for trials and hopefully eliminate all the bugs experienced with any new tank.

The first FV201 prototype by this stage had completed 1,591 miles of running during trials, and then the near-side final drive failed due to problems with poor-quality components. The AVRE(L) prototype had managed a mere 200 miles as part of its workshop trials, and the other prototypes were in various stages of assembly, or only just completing their design stage. For example, the fifth prototype, the FV209 ARV, had still not had detailed drawings of its running gear completed.

At the thirty-third design meeting of the FV201 project, held on 26 July, the universal tank project was declared dead, although its ghost in the shape of a few prototypes would live on, providing a phoenix-like boost for the FV214. This was most notable in the configuration of the gunnery and fire control system that would be fitted to the new tank, except for the stabilization lacked by the FV214.

Even though the FV221 was an expedient to get the chassis into troop trials as soon as possible, it still threw up some problems. If the FV221 was to follow the normal procedure of trials for adoption, then it could push the FV221 in-service date back until about 1955, which would, of course, have a knock-on effect on the FV214 programme. The other choice was to roll the dice and have the first twelve FV221s individually hand-built and then order the production tanks. The gap between the two would be a remarkable six months only. The problem with that approach was that it might not show up faults in the production model. With the desire to get the chassis into service as fast as possible, the latter option was chosen. The first two of the prototypes were to be component testers only and would not in any way resemble the final product. One document states that the second prototype FV221 was dropped to save time. Another document issued in November 1951 states that the second prototype was being built and would fit the first of two Conqueror turrets. The first turret would be assembled as parts became available, while the casting of the second turret would be used for defensive firing trials. The first prototype FV221 was tested at Bovington camp, then due to its non-standard chassis was used to test a gas turbine for a few years, then converted to a variety of roles until finally ending its days as the improvised commentary box at Bovington museum. It was eventually scrapped in the late 1990s as part of the Bovington arena redevelopment.

Preliminary drawings for the FV221 were complete by 26 July 1949, and production drawings were due to be complete by March 1950. The first twenty FV221s were to be manufactured by the Royal Ordnance Factory at Barnbow. The order was estimated to cost between £500,000 and £750,000 for the first twelve.

The trail of the FV221 then goes quiet; presumably everything runs at least close to plan because in September 1953 we find a bulletin listing how the first seven FV221s would be distributed. The British Army of the Rhine (BAOR) was to get one each of the turreted and non-turreted types. The latter types were FV214 chassis fitted with Windsor turrets, which is a large cylinder to provide ballast up to the tank's correct weight and named after Windsor Castle due to its appearance. Middle East Land Forces were to get two turreted tanks, while the RAC centre at Bovington was to get one each of the turret and Windsor types. Finally, the 4/7th Dragoon Guards were to get a fully-operational tank.

Along with the distribution lists came a list of modifications that were to be incorporated into later tanks already but were not included in the seven issued.

First, there was a change in the driver's episcope. It changed from three separate units to one episcope. This change was made to remove a significant obstruction to the driver's arm when he was driving unbuttoned. The bulletin tells the workshops to remove the two side episcopes and block off the hole with wood, although in at least one case, the FV221 delivered to Bovington (licence number 07BA77), it was not done. Indeed, in one picture of the driver unbuttoned you can see he has a distinct list to one side.

One of the first FV221s issued for trials. Of note is the curious muzzle extension, of unknown function, that seems to replace the usual muzzle brake. This attachment is also present on some pictures of the FV221 prototype sent for trials in the Middle East. A possible reason for the attachment is to mimic the length of the Conqueror's gun; after all, this tank was designed to test elements of the FV214.

CONQUERING CANCELLATION

This is a curious item because for many years one of the main ways of telling a Conqueror Mk I from a Mk II was to count the number of driver's episcopes. This document implies that there may only have been two Conqueror Mk Is in existence. These would be the two with the Windsor turrets that would likely have been fitted with full turrets later on. However, checking licence plates in photographs shows that there are at least three more Mk I tanks armed with guns.

Licence plate	Type	Notes
07BA71	FV214 Windsor	One each to BAOR and Bovington
07BA72	FV214 Windsor	
07BA73	FV221	One each to BAOR, Bovington and 4/7 Dragoon Guards. Two to Middle East Land Forces
07BA74	FV221	
07BA75	FV221	
07BA76	FV221	
07BA77	FV221	

Other changes included improvements to the driver's hatch and locking mechanism, fuel system and cooling system. The document also provides a list of faults already known about; most startling are issues with cooling. Losing three gallons of coolant would cause severe overheating. Equally the auxiliary generator could boil the cooling system from cold in just two hours of use, or an alarming forty-five minutes from hot. The report does include some good news, however; as has been mentioned before, it had been impossible to throw a track on the tank.

The two FV221s sent to the Middle East were given to the 14/20th Hussars. By November 1954 they had completed 2,000 miles of running in them, with the only faults being limited to the power plant. This feat earned them several congratulatory telegrams from the chain of command, starting in London at the Ministry of Supply.

One thing seen from time to time is a question of how many FV221s were produced in total. At first, there was a choice of unpleasant decisions for the army. Some 160 hulls were envisioned to be produced as FV221s. However, that would mean either 160 hulls sitting around for the three years it would take to build the turrets – utterly useless if a war was to break out – or produce an extra 160 Centurion turrets that would later be thrown away. It was initially decided that the latter option was the preference. However, in 1952, a financial 'blizzard' was described; it was sweeping through the Ministry of Defence. The Secretary of State for War received several complaints about the costs of the army's new tank from the other services, which were also competing for the same money. For this reason, he held a meeting to decide the future equipment policy. As well as halting the FV4004, a stop-gap attempt to mount an L1 120mm gun on a Centurion as a tank destroyer, this meeting turned its attention to the FV200 series. First, the FV217, a self-propelled 120mm gun in a low silhouette casemate with between 30 and 60 degrees of traverse, was halted. This scheme had originally been intended to follow on from the FV4004 which was seen as a stop-gap measure. From this one can guess that the 120mm gun was the same L1 gun that would be fitted to the FV4004 and FV214. The meeting also confirmed the importance of the Conqueror; however, in light of the costs it was decided to limit production of the FV221 to just ten vehicles, which in due course would be modified to FV214s when the turrets became available.

The development of the Conqueror's turret started in 1950 when on 1 April the Chief Engineer, Fighting Vehicles Design Establishment, finished a document on the shape of the FV214 turret. The armour was calculated as some 13.5in to the front and 7in to the side. Weighing in at 18.5 tons, it held several revolutionary items. First, the turret had a 'fire control' turret on the rear bustle. This could turn up to four times the speed of the main turret and had both the commander and gunner in it, the idea being that the commander could select his target and aim the fire control turret at it. Then the gunner could take over the engagement. When ready, the gunner would flick a switch that would automatically lay the main turret onto the selected target and auto-range the gun.

The hatch on the fire control turret also raised itself vertically for a few inches and allowed the commander to peek under its lip, able to look about while still retaining overhead cover. Most importantly, the movement of the gunner to the fire control turret allowed the turret to have a better ballistic shape. The chief engineer said in his documents that it was heavily inspired by the mushroom shape of the IS-3.

Artist's impression of the original Conqueror turret design, based on the sketch submitted with the paper. The large fire control turret is visible at the back of the turret.

When this document landed at the RAC Centre at Bovington the experts there unanimously denounced the turret. The criticism was less harsh than one might expect. The main reason for Bovington's ire was that while the gunner was engaging the target, the commander had nothing to do but 'twiddle his thumbs'. It was suggested that if the commander was on his own in the fire control turret, he could find the target, take the range and then lay the main turret onto the target, at which point the gunner could take over the engagement, completing the fine laying of the gun. Handing over control of the fine laying left the commander free to start setting up an attack on a new target or even using his cupola machine gun if the situation warranted it. Moving the gunner from the fire control turret to the main turret was judged not to affect the ballistic shape too badly. As it would turn out, protection was lower than the estimates given, but how much less is another enigma of the FV200 series. Documents are wildly contradictory as to exactly how much armour the Conqueror had on its turret front. Some are obviously wrong; one document actually states that the FV214 had 89mm of armour on the turret front. Part of this is likely from the shape and thickness of the turret; British documents had never before had to record a curved variable thickness casting and state what was the front or the side. Even so, there are still contradictory documents. First, we have a plan of the turret design which gives the armour thickness as about 10in. Annoyingly for the researcher, most documents state the requirement of immunity from a Soviet 100mm gun through 30 degrees of arc either side of the gun. One statement of this has a table with estimated penetration numbers given for most Soviet weapons, and the listed number is just over 7in. The issue comes from a later document that states that the required immunity levels were only achieved through 15 degrees either side of the gun, but the plans show a higher thickness of armour than the penetration value over a greater arc of the turret. One solution to this conundrum might be that the estimates turned out to be wrong, or as no document states which 100mm gun was being used, there were two Soviet guns of such calibre covering the rather long life of the FV200 series: the BS-3 of the Second World War, and the D10T mounted in the T-54 series.

There were other steps to be taken to protect the tank. One suggestion was to place the storage bins on the front of the turret and armour the outside walls to 14mm; this would provide a spaced armour layer, as well as protecting the crew's belongings from small-arms fire. This idea was never enacted, although the hull might have received an up-armouring scheme.

Proposals for the FV214, drawn up in March 1950, included a set of 14mm burster plates held at 4in from the hull armour. There had been a similar proposal for the FV201, although how that would have been fitted with the other options, such as the flame gun, is not recorded. These burster plates would be mounted to the tanks and cover the glacis plate. German experience during the Second World War had shown that plates like this, in the style of *schürzen* (spaced armour plates), could be easily damaged or knocked off while driving around. To save money, these were to be manufactured and held as a theatre store. Should war become imminent or even likely, the burster plates could then be issued and fitted. Doing so also had the advantage of keeping the armour as a surprise for the Soviets who would have suddenly found the Conquerors somewhat harder to knock out. There would be no evidence of these ever being actually manufactured and stored or not, as such an item would leave almost no document trail, even in a complete archive which the British lack for the period.

In later years when testing the effectiveness of anti-tank munitions, a Conqueror was used as a target vehicle. The series of tests required spaced armour; therefore a set of spaced protection was scratch built for

The Conqueror range target, up-armoured to test the effect of the extra armour on the perforation performance of the warheads. The turret armour was fabricated for the trials and was never planned for service. It is highly likely that the same applies to the hull armour, although there is just a hint of doubt that it may have been a service store.

the turret. For the hull, the trials report says that '14mm burster plates' were used. The trials report gives no definite indication whether these are the original proposed plates or not, although there is the implication that they were manufactured specifically for the trials.

The gun on the Conqueror was to be known as the L1 120mm gun. A truly huge piece, it tended to bounce around a lot while the tank was in motion, and some concerns were raised about the gun having to be raised to maximum elevation when the tank was moving; for example, if it was unmasking from turret down to hull down. This could have given away its position to the attacking Soviet armoured formations. However, to achieve the required performance of killing the IS-3, it had to be that long. At first the British were looking at standardizing their weapons with Canada and the United States so that they all shared the same ammunition, and thus there was some talk about replacing the 20-pounder with the United States' 90mm gun, although this never came to fruition.

For the L1 120mm, there were steps to standardize as well. Both countries worked together on the United States' T53 120mm gun, used on the experimental T34 tank. In June 1949, both countries decided to stop development, mainly because of the weight of the gun which was some 3.5 tons. The United States started work on a short-term 120mm weapon, the T122, which had a chamber pressure of 17 tons. From then on they would develop the T123, which increased the pressure up to 22 tons. As both countries had decided to standardize on the internal ballistics, Britain decided to design to the higher chamber pressure in the L1.

After both the United States' gun and the British gun were in service, there was a study by the British to see if their guns could fire United States' rounds. The tests involved T116E1 AP shot and T15E3 HE shell, both of which were meant for the T123 120mm gun. It was found to be impossible to load the rounds into the L1 gun, as after the T116E1 AP shot was loaded along with its case the breech block would not close more than halfway across the case base. However, it was found that by filing down the Bakelite cap over the top of the case, the breech could be closed and the gun fired.

When the gun was fired, it produced a fearful shock and blast. The loader had to cling to the turret to avoid being hurled bodily across the turret. The other crew could not use their vision devices for fear of sustaining injury. The blast also caused the auxiliary generator circuit-breakers to pop open every few rounds. Despite the violence of the shot, the gun's run-out and recoil were entirely normal. The United States' powder also left a carbon build-up in the firing pin mechanism, which might have resulted in the misfires that happened on the trials. On the plus side, the powder had a low all-burnt point as there was no muzzle flash observed as the round left the barrel. The T116E1 also produced higher barrel wear. Each AP round shaved 0.0016in off the inside of the barrel, which was about double what a British APDS round would cause.

The L1 was deemed capable of killing an IS-3 at up to 1,000 yards with APDS and at any range with a HESH round. Hitting the target was also seen as an easy task, as the gun was rated as very accurate. The L1 fired two-piece ammunition in the shape of the projectile and case. These weighed either 41.5lb or 60.9lb for the cases for HESH and APDS respectively. The projectiles themselves weighed in at 21.4lb for APDS and 35.3lb for HESH. Thirty-five complete rounds were stored in the

FV214 Mk I, and a trials report on loading suggested that there was room for a thirty-sixth round if modifications were made. The Conqueror used in the trial was the original unarmoured prototype. Of the thirty-five rounds it carried, there were ten projectiles on the turret wall and seven cases on the turntable. All rounds had armoured bins. Dotted around the turntable in the hull were an assortment of cases and projectiles, and on the right side of the hull (roughly where the back of the co-driver's chair would have been in an FV221 or FV201), was a rack with the remaining ammunition. The cases on the turntable were stored base downwards, but this was found to be quite physically taxing for the loader and slowed the rate of fire. The loading trial report suggested that the cases be stored base upwards, which made life a lot easier for the loader.

The report also talked about the L1 gun's safety mechanisms. Initially, the gun had an interlock lever that would only release the breech if the shell had been fully loaded. This lever was a safety mechanism to protect the arm of the loader should he need to reach into the breech to shove the projectile all the way in. However, it was found that the loader just needed to place the projectile in the breech, then he could use the case to push the projectile forward and seat it properly. The problems began when the gun was loaded at more than 10 degrees of elevation. The combined weight of the shell would slide out, meaning that the loader would have to hold the shell in place and fumble about for the interlock lever. It was suggested that removal of the lever would be perfectly safe and mean the gun could be loaded at higher elevations. There was a limit to the elevations at which the gun could be loaded anyway. At full elevation it was impossible to load the HESH round, due to the projectile sliding out of the breech in the time it took the loader to get a case and position it. APDS could be loaded, but it was extremely difficult and tiring due to the angle. Using a ramrod to load was a bit easier but took a lot of time, so it was deemed more sensible to return the gun to level for loading, then re-lay the gun on its target. If the proposals for the removal of the interlock lever and flipping the cases over were accepted, the loading time would have dropped from fourteen to fifteen seconds to just ten to eleven seconds. No hard documentary evidence says whether these changes were made; however, there is a conference report stating that the maximum rate of fire of six rounds per minute was accepted. This would imply that the changes were made on the L1A1 gun, which can be spotted by the presence of the bore excavator.

A Conqueror Mk II: here you can see the changes made from the original sketch. The turret shape is more conical than the dome-like original, and the fire control turret is now just for the commander. An additional hatch has been added to accommodate the gunner in his more traditional position in the turret.

While talking about gun depression, it is a curious thing that the gun could be depressed up to 7.5 degrees; however, the gun would not be amiable at below 5 degrees. This is likely due to the amount of barrel movement in the long L1 gun as the tank travelled cross-country. The extra few degrees of travel would prevent the gun from being damaged if it bounced outside the normal range of elevation.

Originally some twenty Conquerors were planned to be produced in 1953. However, reality fell far short of that, with only five being predicted for 1954. These were to be doled out to various development and other institutions for testing. Twenty-one Conquerors were predicted to be in fighting condition by 1955, although they were primarily for trials use, but could be used to fight off the Russians if a crisis erupted. This prediction was only out by one tank; however, flaws were beginning to show up. There were problems with separation of the sabots from the penetrator on the APDS shot which was affecting accuracy, although some solutions were already under testing. HESH was perfectly accurate, but there were some problems with the amount of debris left in the breech after firing. This would lead to the L1 getting its bore excavator and this fix was predicted to be in place by 1956. Another test being carried out on HESH was the use of a smaller case, which would save some weight. By 1958 these problems had been fixed, then during the training season five Conquerors suffered an engine failure in very short order. This led to the entire fleet being taken out of service until the fault could be found. A specialist investigation was carried out, and the causes of each engine failure were determined. Two were from mechanical failure due to the white metal being found in the oil system, which had ground on the bearings and lubricated parts. One engine had been incorrectly repaired earlier in its life, and two were down to dust contamination.

Further examination of the fleet found that several tanks had high levels of dust in the engine. These were tracked to dirty air filters, but the filter location was also deemed to be partly to blame, with the air intake over the nearside track being the main culprit. Instructions for solving the dust problem were quickly issued. However, the solution to the white metal problem was more difficult. The source of the metal was back at the factory. The engines were not being kept clean while under assembly. To remedy this in the short term, oil filter maintenance was dropped to every 100 miles.

In 1959 the total order of Conquerors dropped to just 150, which was enough for each armoured squadron to have a Conqueror troop.

The Conqueror was still seen as useful, due to its ability to kill any Soviet tank it encountered. In comparison, the Centurions with the L7 105mm were seen as likely to have problems. At this stage, with the L7 still new in service, the only round that could defeat an IS-3 was the 105mm HESH, and HESH-type warheads could be beaten by spaced armour, although the gun on the Conqueror could still punch a hole through the armour with APDS.

The order of FV214 was cut for several reasons, which we will look at in future chapters; however, there is still one more FV200 series vehicle that we need to look at.

Chapter 6

Firepower is Chief

Although there were a great number of FV200 series vehicles, many did not even progress to the design stage. This last FV200 series tank, however, is in some circles a bit of a legend to which much misinformation has been attributed as factual. We are, of course, talking about the FV215.

In some written works the FV215 has the letter 'b' added to it. At least one previous author has stated that the FV215a was an AVRE of some form. In the years that this book's author has been viewing documents on this subject, the tank's designation has only ever been seen written as a plain 'FV215'. There was an early alternative plan of the FV215 which was conventional with its turret amidships and engine in the rear; however, this plan was changed to the more famous

The mock-up of the FV215, representing the logical conclusion to traditional armour development.

rear turret version very early on. It might be that this was what the previous author mistook for the FV215 AVRE and described it as an AVRE. While a document might be awaiting discovery that proves the previous paragraph incorrect, this author has not seen it. For those reasons, we will be sticking with the designation FV215 as referring solely to the Heavy Gun Tank Number 2.

As the name implies, the FV215 was designed to be the successor to the Conqueror. It likely started life sometime in mid-1949 under the designation 'FV Z' and was initially listed as a Super Heavy Gun tank. The requirement for this project was to defeat 6in of armour, sloped at 60 degrees at a range of 2,000 yards! After a year of consideration, the Director General of Artillery (DG of A), Major General Stuart B. Rawlins, answered that there was no practicable gun that could be mounted on a tank that could provide such a huge level of performance. Originally the British were looking at a 155mm gun, standardized with the US, but even this lacked the punch needed. Also, they had test data taken while developing the 6.5in and 7.2in HESH projectiles. The latter presumably belongs to Burney's 7.2in recoilless anti-tank weapon. The information suggests that unless the 6.5in shell hit bare plate, it may not be powerful enough to wreck the target. Also, the reduction in quality of shells was likely during a war, as was the increase of enemy protection levels.

For this reason, the DG of A suggested a new approach. He was sure that a 7.2in HESH shell hitting a tank anywhere, even on its side skirts, would result in a mission kill, blowing off the tank's tracks and rendering its gun inoperable. This approach was termed 'disruption not destruction' in one briefing on the subject. The proposed gun was named the 180mm Lillywhite.

This monster of a gun was to be loaded with a three-piece shell, consisting of a projectile and two charges. The shells envisioned for this monstrous weapon came in three versions. A HEAT shell weighing 50lb with a muzzle velocity of 3,300fps; a 145lb HESH shell fired at 2,740fps; and a final armour-piercing round weighing 71.5lb which was fired at 3,720fps.

Oddly these guns seem to have been 183mm from the start, but it was not until December 1952 that the calibre was officially updated. The gun was designated in service as the L4, which used only a single charge, but a similar HESH projectile weighing in at 160lb. This round was the only ammunition produced for the gun. The charge weighed some 73lb and this propelled the projectile at 2,350fps, generating about 86 tons of recoil force, which was capable of moving the gun mount, which weighed over 4 tons, back 27in.

As usual with this period there is some confusion between differing sources. The Proof and Experimental Establishment at Shoeburyness received a total of twelve L4s, of which six were prototypes, in December 1953, with the first arriving on 18 December. They would receive two more at a later date. After completing trials, these were returned to Woolwich Arsenal in November 1954.

In November 1950 a requirement was issued for a stop-gap vehicle to mount the L4. This would become known as the FV4005, although there is a suggestion in some non-government documents that this design carried the name Centaur. A design was in place by January 1951. If need be, it was considered that it could be in production within eighteen months. This design was to be held as a standby until the FV215 arrived in service.

The FV4005 was a Centurion chassis, mounting the L4 in a large box turret armoured to 14mm to protect against small-arms fire. Although the mount was a turret, it was restricted in its traverse to 45 degrees either side of the centreline. The total weight of the vehicle, which largely determined the thickness of the armour, was 50 tons.

The decision was taken not to produce the tank in early 1951; however, three prototypes were to be constructed. One was an entirely experimental vehicle to test the gun mounting and the recoil forces involved and how they affected the stability of the vehicle. Then with data gathered, two prototypes were to be constructed. The experimental vehicle, known as Scheme 1 or Stage 1, had a gun mounted that could neither elevate nor depress, although it could rotate. As the gun was in a fixed elevation, it was fitted with a mechanical loading assist to help move the giant shells into alignment with the breech, although this arrangement did not load the projectiles as it lacked a rammer; in the later Stage 2 this was removed. Scheme 2 or Stage 2 was to be the real prototype. The gun sight was to be a modified German TZF-12A sight, which was most famously mounted in the Panther tank. The loading system for two gunners was worked out and was described as follows: 'A very simple form of hand-loading which can be operated by two men has been evolved for use in this vehicle.'

The FV4005 Stage 1 pictured when still in the factory after construction. The two men in the background give a sense of the scale of the gun.

The FV4005 Stage 2, now fitted with its very lightly-armoured turret. The armour was just 14mm thick, enough to provide protection against small arms and shrapnel. Of course, with such a massive gun the FV4005 could remain at long ranges and still destroy any enemy tank at which it fired.

During tests, Stage 1 developed some problems with its concentric recoil system, which was an attempt to save space by having the recoil recuperator around the base of the gun barrel. As the Stage 2 used hydro-pneumatic recoil no problems were encountered and the vehicles would eventually fire more than 150 rounds without any problems. In late 1952 the prototypes were tested at Ridsdale gun range by Vickers, and some modifications were found to be needed.

At the end of the project, in August 1957, the three prototypes were sent to various locations. Stage 1 was sent to Shoeburyness Proof and Experimental Establishment, and the Centurion hull returned to active service. One Stage 2 was offered to the Royal Military College for Science, and FVDRE kept the final Stage 2. It is likely that the Centurion chassis was also returned to service, as a single turret was held by Bovington tank museum and at some point was placed on a spare Centurion chassis owned by the museum.

The FV215 was based on the FV200 chassis and shared its Rover M120 No.2, Mk 1A engine, which gave 810hp. This was located some 6in off the centreline in the middle of the tank. The engine output was projected to be able to propel the tank along at 19.8mph. The turret was mounted at the rear of the chassis. The specifications of the tank give the armour value, but as usual, they provide the annoying value of 'to protect from 100mm gun through 30 degrees of arc' that had so plagued research on the Conqueror. The hull armour, however, is listed as 125mm sloped at 59 degrees. In the turret, the commander and gunner sat on the left of the gun, while on the right-hand side one of the two loaders had a .50 machine gun on an AA mount to operate. The loaders had twenty rounds to manage, of which twelve were ready rounds. Between them, they could load at a rate of two to two and a half rounds per minute. The commander had a cupola with an uninterrupted view of 144 degrees. It was also fitted with a collimator which injected the gunner's sight picture into his vision, so he could fire the gun if need be. Due to its sheer size, the gun could only be fired in a 45-degree arc from each side of the hull centreline, or over the rear of the tank. Despite this, the turret had a full 360-degree traverse, but there was a lockout to prevent the main gun shooting to the broadside. The turret traversed at a rate of 12 degrees per second. The main gun had a depression of 7 degrees and an elevation of 15. Oddly, the .30 coaxial machine gun could only depress to 5 degrees. By October 1954 it was realized that the .50 AA machine gun would not be ready in time, so a .30 was to be substituted. There was another idea to give the driver a remote-control machine gun, and such a device was to be trialled on a Centurion. It is likely that this idea amounted to nothing.

At the same meeting, another novel feature of the FV215 was considered. The vehicle was a mantletless variant, which was a new concept in tank design. To test that idea, a cast of the turret front was ordered from Vickers for resistance testing. At the same meeting it was also estimated that the prototype would be finished in June 1957, and troop trials around the end of 1957. By September 1955 the first prototype was under construction, along with spare parts; however, in early 1956, the order placed for two FV215s was cancelled. The closest the project got to a complete tank was the mock-up stage, and it was a full mock-up including internal storage and layout with a mock engine. The reason for this cancellation was down to the army. From the outset, the army was lukewarm about the tank as large-calibre guns have many issues, and there was a new contender for the role of destroying Soviet heavy tanks: the FV4010 (see page 154), which was a modified Centurion chassis armed with a brand-new weapon, the Malkara guided anti-tank missile (see Chapter 13). This revolutionary weapon offered the killing potential of the 183mm L4 for less weight with better accuracy at long range. Although the FV4010 would not enter service either, its idea did tide the army over until a new tank came to fruition.

This new tank started life at the same time as the FV215, only it was identified as the 'FV Y' and was described as a medium tank with a gun to defeat all types of armour. From this, it became the Medium Tank Number 2. In one early design, dated about 1954, the MT-2 had an oscillating turret with a liquid propellant gun. This weapon was a novel concept that had first been suggested in 1947. In such a weapon the projectile is loaded as usual, then the breech is sealed. Liquids are then pumped into the breech and burned to provide the propulsive force to the projectile. There were two main types of this sort of gun: bi-propellant and mono-propellant. The former consists of two different liquids that would chemically react with each other to create the gas. The mono-propellant was a single type of liquid that was pumped into the breech and then ignited by some other means such as a cordite charge or electrical spark. Calculations showed that such a weapon could, if the same size as a conventional weapon, provide much higher muzzle velocities or have the same performance and be smaller. It was this latter attribute that was of interest to the UK designers. To keep the weight of the MT-2 down, the designers were trying to minimize the internal space that needed to be protected by armour.

In July 1954, the Armament Research and Development Establishment (ARDE) began work on both types of gun. The research also included an attempt to make a new improved 30mm aircraft cannon and investigations into what were termed 'bulk-loaded' types. These were replacing some or all of a conventional round's propellant with liquid. Two 20-pounder guns were made, one each of bi-propellant and mono-propellant types, and a 17-pounder used for the bulk-loading trials. In other branches of the bulk-loading testing a 2-pounder gun was used. It managed to get a steel ball up to some 8,000fps; this was done by using 390cc of nitromethane in the case, but otherwise a regular shell.

The bi-propellant design started life with injectors that were located at 90 degrees to each other, but would later have the injectors mounted opposite each other, giving better performance. The first propellant tried

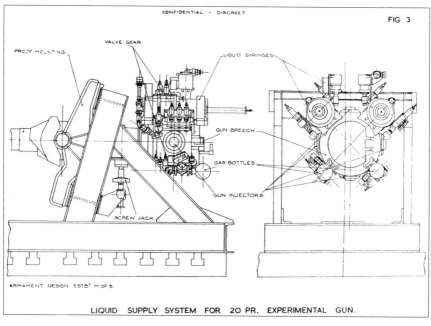

This is the drawing of the 20-pounder liquid propellant gun used for experimental development. This test rig was built and used for several years in an attempt to get a working liquid propellant system.

was red fuming nitric acid with hydrazine as an oxidizer. In December 1954 progress on the bi-propellant was halted as the engineering challenges were taking too long to solve and the system would not be ready in time to be fitted into the tank.

These engineering challenges derived from the chemicals used, and conflicting desirable characteristics needed. On the one hand, inert chemicals are safer and easier to store and use, but more difficult for making a suitable propellant. For the more volatile compounds, the opposite is true. One of the problems encountered was finding steels that contraction be dissolved by the propellants and then creating a method of coating the steel with resistant chemicals that would stand up to the acidic nature.

Work on the mono-propellant gun was seen as much more promising, and this was followed up. The primary way of igniting the propellant was by cordite primers that were fed from a ten-round box magazine and auto-loaded after each shot. Two chemicals were eventually selected for the mono-propellant gun: propyl nitrate and ethyl nitrate. These were settled upon as suitable and were being subjected to toxicity tests; in their liquid form both chemicals caused about the same levels of harm as petrol. However, should the liquid fall onto a hot surface then it would emit extremely toxic fumes. Attempts were made to create an infrared-based warning device, but these failed.

Such was the state of the project when, in September 1957, it was terminated. The principal reason was the non-consistent results of the test firings. Each shot had differing muzzle velocities, even with all things being identical; this was traced back to the internal ballistics and getting an even consistent burn of the liquid. To achieve this, modern solid propellants are manufactured in long rods, which cut up into shorter pieces. These rods have a precise shape, and even an internal structure to ensure the perfect burn. Liquid propellants were just too chaotic and random in the way they burned.

Back in 1955 when it became clear that the liquid propellant gun would not be available for the Medium Tank No.2, a number of conventional designs were looked at for the tank, which had by now received its FV number; we know it today as the FV4201 Chieftain.

Due to size limits, the gun had to fit certain restrictions. First, the breech end of the gun had to fit within the same space requirements as a 20-pounder bag charge gun that had been mounted to the FV4202, which had been built to test various theories relating to the Chieftain's design. In addition, the ammunition, or components of the complete round, was limited to a maximum length of 27in. The performance was required to be able to defeat 120mm of armour, sloped at 60 degrees at 2,000 yards, with APDS. HESH was required to defeat 150mm at 60 degrees. Sixty rounds were specified.

The first gun was to be a weapon standardized with the US, a conventional 105mm gun, which in time would become the 105mm L7. The Tripartite agreement had stated this gun as the main gun of the medium tanks of both countries. However, the ammunition was too long, at some 39in, for the APDS. In addition the gun's performance only just achieved the penetration requirements with APDS but fell short with HESH. A version of this was to create a 105mm bag charge gun, which would reduce the weight of the ammunition by one-third; however, it would raise the same objections due to ammunition performance.

The next option considered was to take a 20-pounder, replace the breech and enlarge the bore to 105mm. This gun fell slightly short of the APDS requirements and had more rifling than was desirable, and again the ammunition was too long.

The FVRDE put forward a new concept: a low-pressure 120mm gun, designed to fire HESH. It was considered that an APDS round could be devised that would get close to the requirements. However, under closer study, it was found that the propellant's 'all-burnt' point was too far up the barrel, which would mean that the round would be very inaccurate. It was at this point that the FVRDE tried a modification to the weapon, and suggested a medium-pressure 120mm gun. The ARDE suggested that the APDS performance would be insufficient, and pointed out that the ammunition would need to be split to fit within the space requirements.

It can be seen from this study the thinking that would lead to the L11 120mm bagged charge gun that the Chieftain would eventually use as its main armament. One question that the ARDE raised was the safety, especially with regard to fire in a bagged charge storage bin. The ARDE suggested a series of trials, which were carried out.

The trials showed that the bagged charges actually reduced risk and it was possible to install a prevention system. This system of water mixed with glycol in a tank surrounding the bag charges was confirmed as the right choice during the Iran-Iraq war. Throughout the war, and particularly in the opening months at the disastrous Battle of Susangerd, many Chieftains were hit and the bag charges set on fire. In earlier tanks, the ammunition would have burst into flames and gutted the tank in seconds. In the Chieftain, the bag charge bins would start to fizz and give off white smoke. The fire would take up to five minutes to catch and destroy the tank. The Iranian tankers appreciated this period as it allowed sufficient time to evacuate the wounded from the tank.

Although the British selected the 120mm bagged charge gun solution, the United Kingdom had been studying the idea of standardization with the United States and specifically their 90mm smoothbore gun. It was decided that the two guns were interchangeable, so the 120mm gun should be proceeded with, therefore if the bag charge design failed, the tank would survive. Furthermore, if need be and the 90mm smoothbore was found to be the superior weapon, the guns could be swapped out at a later date.

At the time there was a shift in British tank design, with the advent of the mantletless tank. The FV215 did not have a mantlet on its design, and two turret fronts had been ordered for firing trials. However, these do not seem to have ever been delivered or the trials carried out. The first versions of the Medium Tank No.2 had a mantlet. Yet the Chieftain that entered service did not. In April 1959 a series of trials were carried out comparing mantletless versions with more conventional layouts. F.H. Lloyd and Co. manufactured two turret fronts, one with and one without the mantlet. As only two were available, the trials did not include HESH and HE-based attacks. These turret fronts had the armour cast to the right standard and thickness, with a dummy gun and cradle. The gun could be elevated and depressed through its normal range to test attacks while the gun was at various degrees above or below 0 degrees. One concern was the lack of mantlet allowing bullet splash to enter the fighting compartment, so two splash guards were designed. One was a pair of nylon mats, 3/16ths of an inch thick, which overlapped in the middle and were fixed to the turret and gun yoke. The other was nylon matting riveted to a metal facing plate. These were tested by firing a .303 Lee-Enfield rifle at the mantletless design, and strangely it was found that the plain nylon mat provided better protection, although both succeeded in preventing splash entering the turret fighting compartment. In the case of the metal-faced version, some of the splash could have fallen into the driver's compartment.

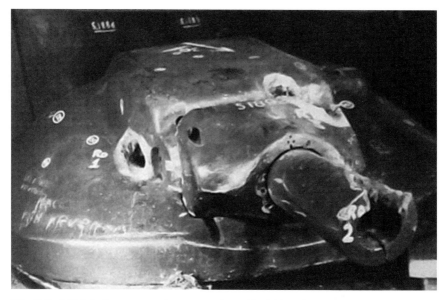

The failed Chieftain gun mantle, as tested on this full-scale replica against a variety of threats.

To see if the guns could be jammed, both arrangements were subject to being shot at by a .303 and .50 calibre Browning heavy machine gun. Unsurprisingly, the .303 shots had no effect. Both turrets had their guns jammed by .50 fire. In the case of the mantletless design, while the gun was at full elevation, a round entered and wedged the gun, which needed a lot of repeated raising and lowering to free it. A hit on the mantlet version jammed the gun so comprehensively that it required the application of some 1,800ft/lb of pressure to release the mount.

Next, the turrets were attacked by far more deadly weapons from a range of just 100 yards. The trials department brought out an SU-100 and began to fire APHE at the turrets, then a 20-pounder firing APDS at the same close range. These impacts deformed the inner face of the turret slightly, creating at worst a slight bulge under an inch high. Finally, the turret roof was used to defend against a 2-pounder gun at 0 degrees. This last trial was to proof test the quality of the armour.

The conclusion of the test was that the mantletless design offered a higher degree of protection, although both could be jammed by a fluke heavy machine-gun hit, and so mantlets would disappear from British tank design until the 1990s.

There is one last piece of information unearthed during the hunt for the FV201, and it comes after the FV201 project was cancelled. In the early 1950s, Nicholas Straussler, the Hungarian tank designer who was responsible for the idea of the DD tank, was recruited by the Hungarian secret service to spy on Britain. So far it has not been proved if he was a double agent or not. He did feed material on technical matters to the Hungarians, much to his controller's unhappiness. The Hungarians were after tactical information, such as unit strengths and so forth. However, in 1955 the Russians approached their Hungarian comrades and expressed an interest in the FV201; how they had heard of it is also part of the mystery surrounding this story. Nicholas Straussler was able to provide a full set of plans, maybe including a turret. The Hungarians promptly sent the plans to the Russians, made a note in their files, and forgot all about the FV201. The Russians also appear to have lost, forgotten or failed to declassify their records about the FV201, and the closest chance we had of finding the FV201's turret fades again.

PART 2

Light Armour

Chapter 7

Light is Right

In 1952 and 1953 the Royal Armoured Corps was facing a problem. Tanks had been slowly increasing in size and weight and were carrying bigger guns, which in turn needed more armour protection to prevent destruction. This upward trend was causing all sorts of problems; for example, there were problems with designing tank transporters for the FV214. The main issue was keeping these under 100 tons in weight.

There is a direct link between the size and weight of a tank and its cost. Heavier tanks not only cost more to build, but they also put increased strain on their components which means these have to be made to higher

Demonstration of the weight problem. Here an FV12001 'Mighty Antar' proves somewhat less potent than the name would imply. The weight of the loaded Conqueror has caused the trailer to slip off the road and it appears to have broken the rear axle.

tolerances, which in turn pushes up the cost. As we have seen, the armed forces of the United Kingdom were facing a financial crisis in the 1950s, with budgets shrinking as Britain desperately tried to drag her economy out of the debts incurred to the United States during the Second World War.

Into this background the new DRAC, Major General Ronald B.B.B. Cooke, began to wonder if something could be done. A lighter tank would be cheaper, but could technology create a light tank that maintained the British edge in quality over the Soviets' greater quantity?

The Fighting Vehicle Research and Design Establishment (FVRDE) at Chobham conducted a series of design exercises on the problem, and finding merit in the idea, produced designs for two vehicles. The first was at best described by the concept of 'What we could build, right now.' At the time when developing new technology, the British tended to do something quick and dirty that they could get into the field as soon as possible, and once that had been completed, they would start work on what they wanted, although not producing the current quick design. This way they could get the best service equipment in the long term but had a stop-gap if the Russians decided to charge over the inner German border.

The FVRDE presented their 'quick and dirty' design, along with the DRAC's thoughts on the tank size crisis, to the RAC conference at the start of December 1953. At the conference, it was termed 'Type A' but was also known as the 'small heavily armoured tank'. It started life much earlier in the year, with the final paper on it being submitted on 27 April.

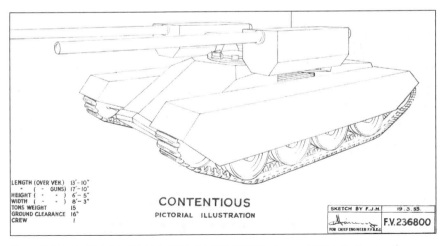

LENGTH (OVER VEH.)	13'-10"
(" GUNS)	17'-10"
HEIGHT (" ")	6'-5"
WIDTH (" ")	8'-3"
TONS WEIGHT	15
GROUND CLEARANCE	16"
CREW	1

CONTENTIOUS
PICTORIAL ILLUSTRATION

SKETCH BY F.J.H.   19.3.53.
FOR CHIEF ENGINEER F.V.R.D.E   F.V.236800

The SMALL HEAVILY-ARMED TANK TYPE A, or FV4401 Contentious, as presented in 1953.

In the final version, it was named as FV4401 Contentious, possibly in anticipation of the amount of disquiet the unconventional design might create among the RAC officers.

Small indeed she was, just 13ft 10in (4.21 metres) long, which was only just longer than some versions of the FV200 were wide! She was also heavily armoured as well, carrying a massive 152mm sloped at 55 degrees for the front. To make it even better protected this was a pike nose so that the armour would be thickened by the compound angle as well. Her sides were less well protected at just 25mm sloped at 5 degrees. Initially the flanks were to be 50mm thick; however, it was found that the nose gave most of the protection needed. A tank, however, she was not, lacking both power traverse and stabilization. From the outset, she was described as a tank destroyer, and that was how she was seen by the delegates at the RAC conference that year.

Before the Second World War, the idea of a one-man tank had been considered overburdening for the lone crewman and duly frowned upon. Equally, there were questions about the lone crewman's morale. However, the success of one-man submarines was considered to have proved the merit of the concept, hence it was implemented for the FV4401. The lone crewman sat in the middle of the tank with a cupola above his head. The 'small' part of the tank's name again is shown by the cupola extending over the engine deck, and the firewall needing to be moulded to the shape of the engine to allow the crewman easy access and egress. The cupola could rotate through 20 degrees either side of the centreline; this permitted the main gun sight, which had been donated from a Centurion, to be aimed at the target. It did mean that the crewman had to twist his body through the 20 degrees as well and is likely the reason for the limit on the traverse. Vertical movement of the sight ranged from –5 degrees depression to +10 degrees elevation. The weapons were mounted on the cupola as well, and several options were considered. The weapons fits were three guided missiles, most likely Malkara, eighteen rockets with a 5in warhead, or a pair of 120mm recoilless rifles. The latter was the only option fully worked out, but it was considered that the others would take minimal work. On the recoilless rifles at first, it was proposed to have four tubes mounted; however, that would limit the combat endurance to just four shots. So two were removed and the remaining pair of weapons fitted with a seven-shot revolver magazine each.

The weapons were ranged by the use of a pair of .50 calibre Browning machine guns. A test rig was constructed and trials carried out. The first problem was to obtain ammunition for the weapon; luckily the FVRDE was able to obtain some from the United States forces based in the UK. With this, they managed to get a spread of 4ft at 1,500 yards in the vertical plane. Engagement time was also measured; this was counted from the first burst of ranging machine-gun fire to the strike of the main armament projectile. To make life even more difficult for the gunner, who was on his first day on the job and therefore utterly inexperienced, the trials staff often gave the wrong range, with the estimated range being out by up to 300 yards plus or minus. This error would cause the first ranging burst to overshoot by a considerable amount. Even with these negatives, the average engagement time was about ten seconds. The cupola also included a special episcope, which allowed the single crewman to look behind him while facing forward and was to be used for reverse driving.

Due to the tiny size of the vehicle, the engine bay was of unusual design. The engine was a Rolls-Royce 'B.81'. At this time, it seemed to be an invented engine, although it would later be realized and enter production. The B.81 was described as an uprated B.80 engine to give 200hp, which could propel the vehicle at 23mph. This engine was offset to the extreme right of the engine bay. To its immediate left only slightly offset from the centreline was a gearbox made by Hobbs Transmission Ltd, with the space beside it filled in part by the 45-gallon fuel tank. Hopefully, the description of this arrangement gives an idea of how cramped the tank was and how the components were stuck in like some form of jigsaw puzzle. Another demonstration of the lack of space is in the crew compartment. Two single-unit air cleaners were fitted on either side of the crewman. Beneath this on the left were the batteries; on the right the C.42 radio set. However, due to space consideration, the controls were mounted just below the air cleaner, while the actual radio set had to be installed separately and further forward.

Suspension and running gear was to be based upon the FV400 series of carriers with the tracks made wider, although the increased weight would mean the components would need to be strengthened. Despite the heavier weight of 15 tons, the ground pressure remained as 11.61psi, which was the same as the FV400. There was a later idea to mount a single set of reloads for the tank, but that would add a ton to the vehicle's weight, and one struggles to see where these shells might have been mounted.

As the name 'Type A' would suggest, there was a second tank, this one unimaginatively named 'Type B'. It was seen as a long-term development, although it shared the same title of small heavily-armoured tank, with the aim of producing a 25 to 35-ton vehicle. At this stage, it was still very nebulous and had only the skeleton of an idea. The armour protection was to be about the same level as the Type A, namely 150mm at 60 degrees. The crew was increased to three, presumably a commander, driver and a gunner, as the gun was listed as being automatically loaded. The notes on this Type B included the idea of automatic gun ranging, which would preclude the use of a ranging machine gun. The main gun was listed as a 'chemical energy weapon in a turret'. This gun was to fire a HESH round, with the same destructive power as the Conqueror's gun. The FV214 was used as the benchmark for determining the accuracy requirement, and the speed of hitting the target. However, the range requirements were decreased to just 1,500 yards.

In 1954 the project for the small heavily-armoured tank was to be included in a new research and development effort known as Project C. This project had an enormous scope; simply anything that could be used in armoured vehicle design, with no set aim or physical characteristics. The only governing ideas were the following:

- The capacity for rapid, prolonged movement without replenishment must receive equal emphasis with offensive firepower
- The destructive capacity of the weapon must be such that the enemy cannot achieve better mobility by a reduction in protection
- The armour provided must force an enemy to mount the largest economical offensive weapon.

The net result of this would be to force the Russians to either continue with conventional tanks and the spiralling costs associated with that, or to mount a research effort of the same level as the sweeping Project C. If the Soviets did follow the British lead then that would cost the Russians dearly, and the British would have the advantage of starting first. Even as the Cold War was in its earliest years, one can see the start of the economic warfare that would eventually contribute to the collapse of the Soviet Union. Project C was so called due to the very young tradition of naming all British tanks with a word beginning with the letter 'C'. However, that was not to last. In the following year, 1955, Project C was renamed, to the name by which it is much better known, as Project Prodigal, although there is no record as to why Prodigal was picked for a name.

Chapter 8

The Prodigal Son

From the note at the 1955 RAC conference about Project Prodigal the trail goes cold, as once again the state of the British archives sabotages the researcher's best efforts. We next encounter Project Prodigal in September 1959 when a presentation on British progress was made to the United States army representatives. Over the previous five years, the small heavily-armoured tank had evolved by a considerable amount. Indeed, it is staggering that the amount of work that was carried out has left so little in the historical record. The presentation was carried out as enough work had been conducted on the project to provide a basic outline of the vehicle's arrangements and capabilities. It was anticipated that a considerable amount of work was needed to provide a final vehicle, but at least now they had a rough idea. This concept had gained a name, also beginning with a C: it was called Contentious. This name was not another rename of Project Prodigal, but a separate development initiative, conducted under the auspices of Project Prodigal and using the earlier tank's name, although it seems to have had little to do with its predecessor.

The tank was light, forecast to be about 20 tons. This weight was achieved by having just two crew, who were located in a survivable pod to which most of the protection was devoted. This pod consisted of the turret and the rear of the hull. Due to the tank's small size, the crew sat in the hull with their shoulders and heads inside the turret. The crew was located on either side of the main gun; at this early stage, this was a 17-pounder. It might be seen as odd to have a tank with a 17-pounder in the late 1950s, but this version of Contentious was nothing more than a test vehicle and was never going to see combat.

The turret itself was of a limited traverse, only being able to rotate through 20 degrees either side of the centreline. Elevation of the gun was through a hydraulic suspension system. The limited traverse and the lack

Above and below: Front and rear views of the Project Contentious idea. This was a mock-up built for testing air-dropping. There were at least two other mock-ups made, both much cruder-looking, so much so that one barely resembled the vehicle. While the shape is closer to the projected vehicle, it is still missing items such as the ribbed armour, and so is nothing more than a mass to be air-dropped in the vague shape of the Contentious.

of elevation for the gun allowed the tank to be fed from an automatic loader. The use of a fixed gun also meant that there needed to be no room to elevate the breech of the gun, again meaning that the roof of the tank could be even lower.

The use of hydraulic suspension to provide elevation of the tank was tested on a heavily-modified Comet chassis, mounting a 20-pounder gun with a limited traverse. During these tests a brand-new technology was trialled: the use of pulsed light, or in modern-day terminology, a laser. The use of a laser speeded up ranging by a considerable margin. As shown earlier, the ranging machine-gun method usually resulted in between eight to ten seconds from first ranging attempt to projectile

Above and opposite: This is the Comet test rig built to test the idea of laying in elevation and with limited traverse. The photograph opposite shows the platform at maximum elevation. It is often labelled as the FV4401 Contentious by modern commentators, and it is implied that the vehicle would somehow have seen service. The total lack of armour protection and the exposed unarmoured fuel tanks show that this is not the case, even if documents from the archives do not prove the point.

strike; with a laser it could be achieved in just two seconds. Under trials, a test rig managed to strike an impressive sixteen different tank targets in one minute. The most advanced part of the technology was the protection. Historically, light tanks like this were usually armoured to be proof against just small arms. However, the Contentious, at least frontally, was better protected than the current British tanks! The glacis plate was just 40mm thick and sloped at 60 degrees.

Behind this, the entire front of the tank was the vehicle's fuel supply, about 4ft in width, followed by another 40mm plate as the forward wall of the crew pod. The two 40mm thick armoured walls were also the fuel tank walls. This arrangement gave enough fuel for about 500 miles of operation. It might seem odd to place the fuel at the front of the vehicle, considering the likelihood of penetration by enemy gunfire, especially so when one remembers the popular story about the cause of the M4 Sherman easily catching fire due to its petrol fuel. This story is demonstrably false and should be roundly mocked whenever it is encountered as the cause of the Sherman's flammability was its inadequately protected ammunition. In Project Contentious, the frontal fuel tank was found to provide added protection. As Contentious was to use a multi-fuel engine, trials were conducted with three fuels – petrol, diesel and AVTAG – the latter being a jet fuel. During these trials, a fuel tank made of 40mm armour was subjected to many attacks from several calibres of gun, up to a 2-pounder and including 30mm ADEN rounds specially designed to destroy fuel tanks. The barrage of projectiles also included Energa grenades and 3.5in HEAT warheads. These were first trials only, and it was intended to work up to 120mm strikes. The fuel tanks themselves were filled to the top in some tests and partially full in others. In the second group, the idea was to provide a fuel/air vapour mixture that was most at risk of ignition. Unsurprisingly, the typical result of penetrating below the fuel line was to cause the tank to spring a leak and the fuel to puddle beneath the hole, at which point it would often catch fire. Although in such a circumstance the risk to the tank was minimal, at worst the vehicle would need to drive a few feet away.

The results of shots into the vapour mixture were more of a surprise. First, the vapour depended on the temperature of the fuel, with even diesel being ignitable above specific temperatures. Around 32 degrees C was considered the critical point. However, when a projectile penetrated the vapour and ignited the mixture, an explosion would occur. This explosion would be extremely weak; less than 100ft/lb. This detonation was such a small explosion that it often could not be heard at the firing-point. The other oddity of the blast was that it would instantly use up all the oxygen, thereby snuffing out any fire. On only two tests were they able to get the fuel in the tank to burn. On shots 109 and 110 the AVTAG inside the tank burned; this was because the impact of the round knocked all the plugs from previous tests out of the tank, causing it to leak heavily and allow air to circulate. Even if this was seen as a problem, there was the suggested fix of filling the tanks with an inert gas to prevent a vapour mixture from forming. The fuel was calculated to give armour protection at the rate of 3in of fuel equals 1in of armour plate. In total this gave the front of the Contentious about 25in of armour!

At the time of the submission of the report, an improved design of the fuel tank was being worked on. It added a rear fuel tank and broke the front fuel tank into three compartments. The largest fuel compartment ran at a 60-degree angle from the floor of the tank to the wall of the crew pod. This container was used as a reserve tank, using fuel from the rear tank and the smaller frontal compartment first. Doing so kept the protection levels and minimized the weight shifting as the tank used its fuel. To further protect the large tank, a smaller layer of foamed plastic was provided, which would seal holes in the large tank.

However, the protection wizardry had not ended with the novel idea of using the fuel as armour. The front glacis was also ribbed. The idea behind this may have gone back to the Second World War. During the Normandy campaign many tank crews up-armoured their tanks with track links and other items they could lay their hands on. The British War Office undertook a study into this practice. One particular officer was heard to give a detailed explanation of how the rough edges of the tracks caused the shots to break up. The study did investigate all these claims and found that the improvised armour had absolutely no effect when mounted on the hull of the tank. When fitted to the turret the additional armour actually ran the risk of unbalancing the turret, causing excessive wear, and slowed the turret traverse slightly. In a bout of common sense, the War Office quickly realized that although it had no physical benefit, it did give a boost to morale. Also, it was effectively impossible to ban and would give the impression of remote staff officers trying to meddle and lower the protection of the front-line soldiers.

The ribbed armour was an attempt to develop a type of armour that would cause the incoming shot to break up. To test this idea in August 1948, a plate had 2in-thick IT80 armour with ribs welded onto it. Then at a range of just 126 yards, a 6-pounder APCBC was fired at the target, which was sloped back at 30 degrees. To find out how effective the plate was, it was weighed and then the equivalent thickness of the solid plate, for the same weight, was calculated. With this number in hand, the critical velocity of the 6-pounder was taken from previous knowledge of the gun. The critical velocity was the muzzle speed needed to beat the thickness of the plate. Now with the velocity known, shots were fired against the ribbed plate at above and below the critical velocity to see their effect on the target. Results of the trial were inconclusive; the ribbed plate gave about the same levels of protection as a solid plate of the same weight. However, the report had one important note. Due to the cost of manufacturing the plate, the cheapest option had been taken in construction: a regular sheet of armour that had the ribs welded to it. Because of this, the welds became points of failure under the impact stresses. The tests also failed to use any chemical warhead rounds, such as HEAT or HESH.

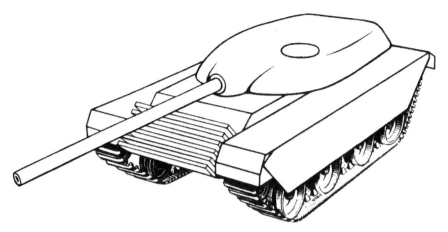

The sketch of the Project Contentious vehicle; here can be seen the ribbed armour that would contribute so much to its protection.

Research into this form of armour continued, although several of the documents are missing. One of the surviving ones is from August 1956. During this trial, a much better set of armour was subjected to a ferocious pounding. Seven plates of cast armour, manufactured by F.H. Lloyd and Co., with the ribs being part of the casting, were shot at by a variety of shells. These included 120mm HESH from an L1 gun and HESH rounds from a 25-pounder field gun. To test the effect of solid shot, AP Mk 5 and APCBC Mk7T was fired from a 17-pounder. A variety of rib dimensions had been included in the samples built to test their effectiveness and to see if there was an optimum arrangement. The ribs were manufactured consistently on an individual plate but varied in measurements on different plates. The ribs varied from 0.75in to 1.25in thick and from 3in to 7in inches in height. The spacing between each rib was also varied from 2in to 4in.

The trials found that the most critical factor seemed to be the height of the rib. This result was shown by a test of the same rounds against the same rib width and spacing, with only the rib height being different by 2in. This height increase managed to drastically alter the angle at which it was immune to attack from the 25-pounder shell by about 30 degrees. To test their findings, one of the plates was fired at with a 120mm HESH round, while the angle was set to 0 degrees. The HESH round penetrated the plate and blew it to pieces. Another advantage of the ribbed armour was that it was more robust than the solid plate and a covering of spaced armour. It also confirmed the earlier test, pointing out that ribbed armour was at least equal to the solid plate, if not slightly superior against solid shot. It was suggested that a Centurion fitted with ribbed armour could be made immune to 25-pounder HESH and the Conqueror immune to 120mm HESH, both of which would currently defeat the glacis plates on the tanks. One critical point was that the plate needed to face towards the enemy and be sloped at over 40 degrees to achieve the results. The Contentious hull was sloped at 60 degrees, and due to its limited traverse, the hull should nearly always be pointing towards the enemy for maximum protection.

The Contentious also included protection against other forms of attack, the main one being nuclear.

At the time the idea of a limited war, with no or minimal use of nuclear weapons, had not been considered, and it was thought that should the Third World War ever start both sides would go straight to full force, including nuclear weapons. Because of this, it was fully expected that the Contentious would need to fight on a nuclear battlefield. Here speed and mobility became important again, allowing units of tanks to be spread out further to avoid a nuclear attack. Then when the time was right, the forces could rapidly concentrate and fight. This need for dispersion is another reason for the long endurance required of Contentious. To allow the Contentious to operate in a radiologically contaminated area, the crew was to be provided with a closed-circuit television system.

The low silhouette of the vehicle would give some protection against blast, and even a small thickness of armour would protect against the thermal effects. However, the significant threat was radiation. Ionizing radiation that would affect the crews of tanks comes in two forms that are dangerous. Alpha and beta radiation can be relatively easily stopped; however, gamma radiation and neutrons have much higher penetrative power. Luckily the armour found on contemporary tanks such as the Centurion or the Conqueror was able to cut gamma radiation by a significant factor, it was suggested to about a factor of ten. However, the Contentious had much lighter armour; so how would it fare against a barrage of gamma radiation? Some 40mm of armour would cut radiation by about 50 per cent. Therefore the crew inside Contentious, protected by two sheets of 40mm, would be receiving some three-quarters of the outside dose, which was considered sufficient. Medium and higher-energy neutrons, however, could pass right through any thickness of armour and still have an ionizing effect on the human body. To protect the crew, scientists worked out a way of using hydrogen for this purpose. The hydrogen molecule is the closest in weight to a neutron's mass. The technique was to have the neutron impact onto lots of hydrogen molecules; each impact would, in turn, scrub off some of the energy of the neutrons until it was slowed enough to enter the thermal range, whereupon the armour could absorb the energy. To this end, the crew compartment was coated with 6in to 8in of polythene and boron lining, which was found to provide a twenty-to-one reduction in radiation. It also had the advantage of limiting the effects of any penetration of the armour, restricting the stream of spall and debris to a very tight cylinder.

At the time there was a lot of interest in the West regarding using their advantage in nuclear science by using fractional yield nuclear warheads for anti-tank work. Blasts as low as 1 ton could be created, and it was believed that the Russians could not produce such small warheads. The advantages of having nuclear protection would mean the need for an increase in accuracy of the tactical atomic weapon as the warhead would have a much smaller lethal area of effect. The radiation proofing also allowed the tank to employ its own anti-tank nuclear warheads at much closer range than without the lining. Early in 1960, the scientists working on Project Prodigal started to look with interest at the United States' 152mm gun-launcher, and more specifically the Shillelagh missile. The idea was attractive, and the projected UK weapon would carry a 6in 15lb HEAT warhead, which would be mounted on a 50lb guided missile that would have a high speed. The downside was that the huge HE round would be too big for supporting fire. The FVRDE proposed a solution whereby the breech of the weapon was mounted inside the turret like a normal gun, but instead of a barrel, there was a simple launching rail. That way it could fire anything from a 3.5in to 4in HE missile, all the way up through the 6in ATGM to an 8in fractional yield nuclear warhead. It was envisioned that the size of this anti-tank nuclear rocket would require the warhead to be placed onto the rail first, then the body of the missile loaded onto the rail and the two sections joined in place.

Such a missile solution was rejected for a variety of reasons. These included the cost of the missile, and training to cover the longer more detailed training period for gunners. The concept of line-of-sight riding missiles was also seen as problematic, due to ground cover obstructing the flight of the missile. However, it was noted that the latter could be fixed by the development of a homing warhead, where the missile was fired at an angle upwards, and after a climb-out the homing missile would take over and aim itself at the target, an envisioned flight profile that is almost identical to missiles such as the modern-day Javelin ATGM. However, at the time, there was not even a glimmer of an idea on how to create such a homing warhead, but the concept was included for completeness sake. The biggest reason for the rejection of the missile solution was the rate of fire. As has been stated, the Contentious test rig had managed to hit sixteen targets within a minute; a feat that no ATGM stood any chance of achieving. In addition, to reach 2,000 yards an APDS round would take almost one and a quarter seconds. In comparison, early missiles such as the Malkara took about fourteen seconds. Even a fast missile such as the Shillelagh would take eight seconds.

As the 17-pounder was obviously too weak to be used for a front-line weapon, work was untaken by the Royal Armament Research and Development Establishment (RARDE) in Fort Halstead to look into methods for the automatic loading of a sufficient weapon. The weapon specifications were provided by General Staff Operational Requirement (GSOR) 1016; although either gun or missile could have met the requirements as issued, RARDE worked on the principle of using an L11 120mm gun. It may be that this led to the L11A4 version of the 120mm gun that was built for evaluation purposes. The choice of an L11 meant that existing stocks of ammunition could be used, and the use of bag charge simplified the way the gun cycled, as it did not need to eject a spent case. The gun itself was to have 2 degrees of movement in all planes for fine aiming, but otherwise the method of laying was the same as Contentious. As this weapon and loading mechanism were destined for a light vehicle, it was to make extensive use of high-strength steels and special light alloys. Despite this, the mounts for the main gun would be problematic; to keep the trunnion pull down to the same levels as a 105mm L7, a muzzle brake was needed. The rapid rate of fire might, it was thought, cause obscuration problems, with the blast from the gun blocking quick observation of shots and laying the gun. It was, therefore, suggested that the blast be piped and vented to the rear of the tank. The gun itself was designed to recoil only 12in to 18in. The requirements stated that a minimum of thirty rounds were provided but sixty was desirable, with the ability to switch between HESH and APDS at will. The ammo was desired to be split between twenty rounds of

APDS and ten of HESH. To keep things simple the RARDE engineers tended to stick to the lower ammo limit of about thirty rounds in the seven schemes they drew up. Further, and most impressively, the gun was to have a maximum rate of fire of thirty rounds per minute! The mechanical movement inside the loading systems was provided by Fenlow push-and-pull hydraulic rams.

Above and opposite: Artist's impression of some of the Project Prodigal designs. Each vehicle has a different automatic loading system. The vehicles themselves were only roughly sketched on the detailed loading system plans in tiny images to give a rough idea of what each one would look like.

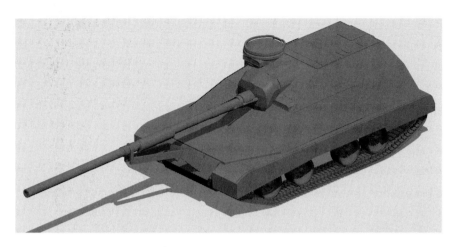

The loading systems included a train feed, where containers linked to each other literally formed a train and were rotated around at a speed of 5fps. Each round was stored nose to tail, and as the required round passed over a loading tray, it dropped into the aperture and then was rammed into the breech. There was a belt-fed version that had a belt of HESH and a belt of APDS that could feed to the breech. The drum feed version had two drums, one above and one below, taking up the entire width of the vehicle, which is given as 8ft 1in. Twenty of the shorter APDS rounds could be stored as in a drum magazine, with their tips towards the centre and the base at the rim of the drum. However, the HESH rounds were longer and so only ten rounds could be carried; these were slanted at an angle to enable all ten to be placed in the drum. One of the designs, the chain drive version, had a variant in which it used a case for the propellant in place of a bagged charge; this was described as a stub case.

Strategic mobility for Contentious was of concern. No work had been done on carrying AFVs over a few tons by air before. Even the lower weight of the Contentious at 20 tons was utterly unknown territory. On top of that, the army wanted to know if they could drop the AFV from an aircraft. In the final months of 1956 work began between the

Another picture of the Project Contentious mock-up. This photograph clearly shows how the beams were to be fitted to allow the impact to be transmitted to the hull, not the delicate suspension.

Royal Aircraft Establishment (RAE) and the FVRDE to see if the current transport aircraft, the Beverley, could carry the Contentious, and indeed air-drop it. After the initial investigation suggested it should be mathematically possible, a project was initiated on 18 July 1957. At this stage of progress, the idea of the project was not to develop a piece of equipment for service use; rather just to test the theory and technology behind the concept.

As a starting-point, the technique used for ejecting supply platforms out of the planes was selected. However, as the method did not use a supply platform or roller conveyor, it saved a lot of weight from the load, which would have detracted from the plane's performance. During landing, the idea was to use the rigidity of the Contentious' hull to absorb the landing forces. However, damage to the suspension could render the vehicle combat incapable. The answer was to mount beams running along the underside of the hull parallel to the tracks. These extended below the bottom of the track line. The protruding beams would transmit the shock of landing directly to the hull. As another measure to control the landing airbags were used, which would inflate after leaving the aircraft and give a cushioning effect. Trials carried out with weights up to 17.5 tons gave a landing velocity of 35fps. This speed was deemed acceptable, and a trial with a dummy of the Contentious was carried out. The Contentious was fitted with an engine, radio and gearbox, all of which survived the landing with no damage.

Chapter 9

Reach for the Skies

In 1960 air mobility was again considered for Project Prodigal, this time in the tactical sense. The paper looked into the idea of making the tanks fly, or rather what performance of limited flight ability would be useful to an armoured vehicle. The study concentrated on reconnaissance vehicles, as they would gain the most benefit from taking to the air for short periods, although the study did suggest that, later on, making heavier vehicles fly would also be of use. The study concentrated on a vehicle about the size of a Daimler Ferret, and indeed most of the illustrations that came in the paper show a Ferret skimming over hedges and trees. From a study of obstacles and terrain features, it was found that the flying Ferret needed to be able to jump under its own power, to a height of about 10ft and distance of 30ft, to clear the majority of obstacles. More substantial obstacles such as trees and forests would need a free flight ability of about 150ft altitude, which the study suggested should come in the second generation. The paper also called for the ability to descend, safely, from a height of 20ft, mainly because there was no ability to look before leaping, and so what might be a 10ft obstacle on one side might be considerably more on the other. Water features would require no real change in height but would need to travel some 1,500ft distance.

These ideas were enshrined in 1960 as General Staff Operational Requirements (GSOR) 1009. The GSORs mark a change in how the army acquired and developed its equipment. From this point, the War Office would issue a policy statement (WOPS) on how future wars were to be fought, and the General Staff would then issue a requirement for equipment to meet these policies. This equipment would then be developed. It stems from a demand from the Treasury to provide an accurate forecast for the financial costs of weapon development over the longer term. GSOR 1009 called for a vehicle named the Ground Air Scout Car (GASC). It mostly followed the Project Prodigal paper's requirements, apart from having the additional condition of no vulnerable flight components. It had a requirement of 50mph flight speed, but 130mph was desirable. On the ground, it should have the same level of mobility as the Ferret armoured car, and 150-200 miles of ground range. The crew was to be a minimum of two, but three was considered desirable. One of the crew should be the driver/pilot, and it was highly desirable that the driver not have to be of the same level of skill or ability as the pilot of a conventional aircraft.

Conversion to flying mode should be possible from either a bogged position or while on the move. One first idea to solve this requirement appeared in 1961, and then again in 1962 when the RAC had a sudden revival in interest in light one-man aircraft, a piece of prototype equipment was displayed at the RAC conferences. In the notes, it was listed as the Wallis autogiro. It was intended to be a one-man flying scooter able to move about for liaison and reconnaissance. The vehicle could be driven on roads or take to the skies as needed. The suggestion was that a controller for a guided missile could be mounted. The same model of autogiro shot to fame in 1967 as 'Little Nellie' from the James Bond film *You Only Live Twice*. The GASC was projected to start coming into service in the first half of the next decade, between 1971 and 1975. It was not seen as a replacement for the Ferret, more to complement it.

At the 1960 RAC conference, there were a lot of presentations about potential vehicles that could be used by the army in the long-term future. These included flying platforms, flying saucers, VTOL (vertical take-off and landing) aircraft, GASC, GAV, hovercraft, ground-effect machines and zero ground pressure vehicles. The latter is a very odd-sounding craft, which caused some confusion. Luckily a member of the FVRDE, Mr D. Cardwell, was on hand to explain it. He told a story of a truck driver that was seen heading along the M1 motorway. Every so often he would pull over on the hard shoulder, run around his truck smacking the sides with an iron bar he kept in the cab, then leap back into the driver's seat and continue on his way. Eventually, he caught the attention of the police, and after following the truck for a while and seeing the truck driver's peculiar routine they decided to stop him. The policeman said: 'You should not stop on the M1 anyway, but do tell me, why do you keep beating the sides with an iron bar?' To this the truck driver replied: 'This, as you can see, is a one-ton truck; I have thirty hundredweights [about 1.68 tons] of budgerigars on board and I have to keep them flying!'

From here Mr Cardwell began to explain the problems around the GASC. He did point out that a GASC was possible, as nature had already built one in the shape of the horse. All that was required was a horse with more performance. The way Mr Cardwell compared the performance of aerial vehicles was by measuring the downward efflux measured in feet per second. The higher the efflux, the more fuel needed to run the device, but the more compact the solution (and thus the better for design). He gave a few examples, one being a helicopter having an efflux of about 80fps, ducted fans about 500fps and a powered jet lift, like those fitted to the Shorts S.C.1, about 2,000fps. Another part of the problem facing the designer was fuel consumption. The example he gave was a ducted fan which would consume its own weight in fuel every ten minutes. Equally, the same engine could not be used in the air as on the ground without considerable difficulty. This problem was because on the ground the GASC would require some 50-100hp from the engine, but in the air 200-300hp. Finally, the aircraft safety principle was imposing some weight penalties. This principle is that should a significant flight component fail, the crew could still safely make a landing.

Despite these technological challenges, five companies had been given a £4,500 contract each to carry out a feasibility study the year before the conference. A further two companies carried out similar studies voluntarily. Oddly, at the RAC conference of 1960, a slightly different sequence of events was portrayed, with the statement that nine companies had been approached and eight had turned in designs.

The requirements had been carefully worded so that an aircraft could not be used. The GSOR, however, left enough leeway for the designers to exercise their imagination. The designs fell into three broad groups. The first was the hopper, able to jump into the air for some ten seconds, up to fifty times. These could be split or combined into shorter or longer jumps as needed, as long as the total endurance did not exceed 500 seconds. Some had attachments for use as a hovercraft to cover the water obstacle. Only two of the designs were hoppers. There were four in the second group, using ducted fans to operate rather like low-altitude, low-speed aeroplanes. Finally, the last group were much closer to aircraft and had full flight abilities. One used helicopter-style rotor blades and one had folding wings. This presentation had models built of all the solutions. These were filmed; however, so far as has been found, none of the footage or stills has survived to show us what these ideas looked like. A full list of companies involved in these designs is also missing.

We do, however, have details of some of the submitted designs. The first was from Bristol Siddeley Engines Ltd, who were one of the voluntary entries. Their entry, the P.S.101/2, was a 3.5-ton vehicle with four-wheel drive. The lift was provided by a pair of large-diameter contra-rotating fans. The wording on the description suggests that these were stacked on top of each other. Air intakes for these were on the sides of the vehicle to improve stability. The fans were of hollow steel with the exhaust piped through them to prevent icing of the blades. The P.S.101/2 was powered by three A129 turbines and could fly at about 60 knots up to a ceiling of 10,000ft. In October 1961 a new version was submitted; this was to cut down on the substantial development costs which the War Office found unpalatable. The revised design had a service ceiling of just 10ft and just ten minutes of endurance. Bristol Siddeley had misread the War Office's intentions as it was not only the cost of development but the whole concept of a flying vehicle that was in disfavour. Such a flying vehicle would need a highly-trained pilot and men with the physical and mental abilities to be a pilot were considered rare, and even then in need of extensive, expensive training. Besides, the high unit cost of a flying vehicle and the need for forward bases were frowned upon.

Also, Bristol Siddeley submitted a 4.5-ton vehicle they called a Freight-Lifter. The vehicle was able to lift about 2,500lb with two hours' flying time at 50mph. It was a two-axle, six-wheeled vehicle which required six 1,000hp engines.

On 5 February 1962, Handley Page gave a presentation on a Ground/ Air Vehicle, although the details of what the arrangements of this vehicle were, or even what it was called, are not recorded. None of these ideas matched the army's thoughts though. The company that did come closest was English Electric, soon to become BAC. Named P.35, it soon became known as the 'Jumping Jeep'. In February 1962 a full feasibility study was ordered and £62,000 allocated. BAC managed to come in under budget, only spending £54,000. In July 1964 a complete development project, with the aim of producing four prototypes, was ordered. However, gaps in the original feasibility study had caused some problems. First, the FVRDE had decided against the original engine. The first versions of the P.35 had been powered by a pair of Italian-produced Meteor Alpha 6 engines, giving 320hp each. These had been rejected by the FVRDE due to them being of foreign manufacture, which raised concerns about supply. Also, technology had moved on and new data about the science behind the design had been discovered. A small design group was convened, and they updated the original feasibility study, submitting their report in May 1965.

There was a fundamental difference between BAC and the government on the nature of the financial arrangements for the contract. BAC wanted a Cost-Plus contract, while the government wanted an Incentive-Price version. These negotiations took over five months and, in the end, the government accepted BAC's terms but had strict controls. These controls were provided by breaking the project up into three stages. After each stage, the government could review the progress and either release the funding for the next phase or cancel the contract. Total projected costs of the project were about £1.1 to £1.3 million, which included a contingency fund.

With the Meteor Alpha 6 no longer available for use, another engine had to be selected. Rubery Owen were chosen to provide an alternative engine with their BRM V-8 producing 250hp, and it was acknowledged that this would mean a drop in jumping performance. However, permission for the engine development was not issued until some six months after the project had commenced at BAC. This, in turn, caused further knock-on effects as Rubery Owen has racing interests for which they prioritized research work over the government contract.

One of the promotional pieces of artwork that BAC included in their P.35 presentation. This shot is showing the P.35 driving along like a standard truck. Later shots would show it hovering or even in mid-jump.

Despite all these setbacks and problems, Stage 1 was completed in September of 1966. During this research period, many of the sub-assemblies of the vehicle had been assembled and tested. From this, we can gain a good idea of the capabilities of the P.35 and how it worked.

In shape, the P.35 most resembled a pick-up truck, about 16ft long, with the cargo space filled with the twin engines. The jumping performance was provided by four banks of three 23in fans, for a total of twelve units. One bank was located on each side of the vehicle. The energy was stored in flywheels rotating at 38,000rpm. In the first version of this vehicle only two flywheels were provided, but later research showed that these would not provide sufficient storage. In the final design, two flywheels were provided for each bank of fans. Both engines, reinforced by the energy taken from the flywheels, would allow each fan to be spun

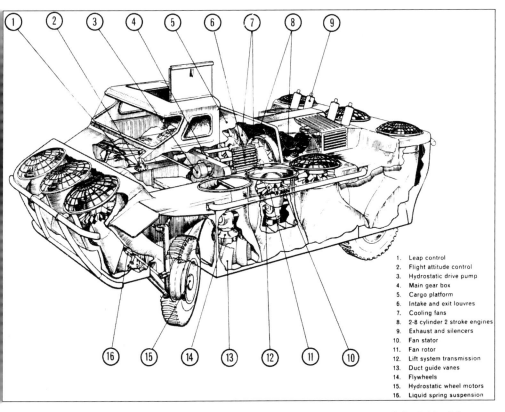

1. Leap control
2. Flight attitude control
3. Hydrostatic drive pump
4. Main gear box
5. Cargo platform
6. Intake and exit louvres
7. Cooling fans
8. 2-8 cylinder 2 stroke engines
9. Exhaust and silencers
10. Fan stator
11. Fan rotor
12. Lift system transmission
13. Duct guide vanes
14. Flywheels
15. Hydrostatic wheel motors
16. Liquid spring suspension

Another extract from the presentation, this time showing a cutaway of the P.35. Of note is number 14, the flywheels that stored so much of the power for jumping. There would be two of these for each bank of three fans.

up to a peak speed of 2,200rpm. After the initial burst of energy, the fans would need less power as they had overcome inertia. This burst of vertical thrust would propel the P.35 about 12 to 14ft into the air in just five seconds. Doing so would slow the flywheels down to about 25,000rpm. The rest of the energy stored in the flywheels would be used to provide more thrust to allow a graceful descent. Once on the ground, only one engine would be used to move the 2.75-ton vehicle, while the other engine could be used to recharge the flywheels.

The balancing was done automatically by a mechanical gyro that would boost or decrease the thrust for each fan to keep the P.35 level during its jump. There is the obvious question of why not use rockets, which are mechanically simpler. The answer was the requirement to provide some fifty jumps. To do so the rocket fuel would weigh more than the vehicle itself, and there were safety concerns for using large volumes of hazardous fuel. Also, a rocket's signature upon firing was quite large and easy to acquire visually and follow through its leap. In comparison, the stored energy approach would have had a brief puff of dust when the fans were triggered and nothing else. The use of fans also allowed the P.35 to act as a hovercraft, clearing obstacles about 1ft in height. The Jumping Jeep carried 40 gallons of fuel, which would give a road range of 200 miles with a top speed of 50mph, 6 miles in hovercraft mode or fifty jumps, or any combination of these.

The chassis and hull were made from light alloy panels with corrugated steel inserts to provide the strength. Other components were steel or where possible light alloy. The fan blades were made from a substance called Flomat moulding dough, which was formed onto a steel rod. There had been problems with quality control in obtaining sufficiently strong steel rods for the high-speed rotations needed, but these had been overcome during Stage 1.

The load capacity of the vehicle was placed at about 500 to 600lb. The load could be increased to 850 to 1,000lb with a corresponding decrease in jumping performance. There was a suggestion that a lightly-armoured version could be created with 6mm armour around the cabin, which would consume about 500lb. The remaining weight would provide enough spare capacity to mount one of two weapon options. Either a GPMG and 2,000 rounds or a pair of Vickers Vigilant missiles could be fitted. In the BAC brochure on the project, a rack of three Vigilant missiles are shown mounted on a platform above the engine.

The armoured version of the P.35, rather hopefully armed with three Vickers Vigilant missiles. The main point of note is that the cab has been replaced by an armoured version. This armoured box would surround the crew space and provide a modicum of protection against enemy action.

As Stage 1 had progressed, various nations had expressed an interest; as well as Canada, both France and Australia had been paying attention. The US in comparison had gone more for the full free flight capabilities and spent some $10 million on their different projects before abandoning the idea altogether.

With Stage 1 complete, BAC was ready to start Stage 2 by constructing a mock-up of the cabin and front of the vehicle, which would include all the controls and at least one complete fan unit. However, the War Office did not approve Stage 2. The problem that caused the cancellation of the P.35 was not technical; indeed, one government official said that the project had made 'steady if unspectacular progress'. The problem was the cost of each vehicle. The army had been interested when the P.35 was forecast at £25,000 pounds. During Stage 1 the forecast unit cost had risen to around about £45-50,000, with around £4,500 for each engine.

In comparison a Ferret scout car came in at £7,000, a two-seat helicopter about £20,000 or a Westland Scout around £75,000. Another measure was that each P.35 would cost the same as a brand-new Centurion tank. This projected unit cost should also be viewed in the light of the times. As usual with the British army, the Treasury was cutting the defence budget. There was also no guarantee that the cost per unit would not rise further. Thus the P.35 project was cancelled in October 1966.

However, before that, there was one other last fling with the idea of ground/air vehicles. Briefly, in late September/early October of 1966 a project called the Clodhopper was considered. This design had come from David Budworth Ltd. Originally it had been designed as a private venture and first appeared in 1964. The design relied on four Blowfly turbines to power the eight fans. Each turbine provided 250hp. Unlike the P.35, it could fly up to an altitude of 1,000ft for about fifteen minutes. The cost was said to be about £10,000 per unit. The plan submitted in support of the Clodhopper was much more basic than the P.35 and was even described as 'having the aura of the wild inventor' about it. Matters were not helped by the submitted brochure suggesting that it could be made amphibious or, should longer endurance and speeds be required, include the fitting of wings.

At the time the Ministry of Aviation was asked for their engineering opinion. They flat-out refused to conduct an assessment of the vehicle. In addition, there was significant concern about the ability of the company to develop the engine to sufficient standards, which led to the Clodhopper being ignored.

By 1966, with the failure of the P.35 and Budworth Ltd having some success in developing turbines, including an impending trial in a helicopter in Germany, the Clodhopper was hastily reviewed. It was deemed viable but would need some input from an external source to make the engine work, yet the government did not want to put forward the financial support. The idea of British Petroleum being brought in was floated to all parties. BP had a fleet of tankers around 1,000 strong. A small development contract would cost them a small amount but give huge returns using the engine in their ships. BP was on the verge of giving David Budworth's just such a development contract when the British army's greatest enemy struck again. Tax laws were changed by the Treasury; this drastically cut BP's spending margins and consigned the British interests in ground/air vehicles to history.

Chapter 10

The Last Success

At the start of May 1960, the Weapons Development Committee began to look at light armoured vehicles. The DRAC at this time, Major General Gerald C. Hopkinson, was asked for a paper on the matter and the current position and views of the RAC. This paper was submitted and discussed in December, and the WDC suggested that the DRAC liaise with other departments on the subject and re-submit in December 1961. As we have seen, there was a change to how the army obtained its equipment. The first policy statement (WOPS No.1) was for an air-portable armoured fighting vehicle (APAFV). This would, in time, develop into the requirement for both an APAFV and an air-portable reconnaissance vehicle (APRV). These would result in GSOR 1001, which would later be re-worked and re-issued as GSOR 1006 for the APAFV. GSOR 1010 was to be the APRV. WOPS No.2, however, addressed ground-based reconnaissance vehicles, but initially did not have a GSOR associated with it.

The armament system for this new family of vehicles was enshrined in GSOR 1012, written in February 1961, which would have far-reaching effects for the British army.

It had all started a few months earlier at the fifth tripartite armour conference at Fort Knox in September 1960 when a discussion on heavy automatic weapons was carried out and, from this, the requirement for a light vehicle weapon system was agreed upon. However, the agreement, and thus the GSOR, lacked mention of the weapon needing to be automatic. The way the requirement was worded, it suggested to the designer that a single-shot, high-performance weapon would be a better design. The basic requirement was for six successful engagements per minute at 1,000 metres. At the tripartite infantry conference in October 1960, an identical requirement was issued, only that it should be for infantry use. To this end, the United States started work on the Vehicle

Rapid Fire Weapon System (VRFWS), which could be dismounted for infantry use. Because of the use of the weapon system on a ground mount, the United States imposed a weight limit of 160lb due to that being the limit of the M3 tripod. From the VRFWS the United States issued a requirement for the VRFWS-S, the last 'S' being for 'successor'. This weapon was the Thompson Ramo Wooldridge 6425, often shortened to the TRW 6425, which was a 25mm weapon with dual-feed belts. The UK did order and presumably pay for one of these guns, spares, drawings and 1,000 rounds of ammo. The order was placed on 23 August 1965 and had a cost of $46,452.

In Britain, the GSOR was issued without the rapid-fire as part of the description. The DG of A, the outgoing Major General Edward J.H. Bates, asked for a full assessment of the GSOR by the Department for Armaments Research and Development Establishment (DARDE) by mid-September 1961. This request turned out to be impossible due to significant gaps in available data on light cannon lethality, which needed trials to be conducted. However, an interim assessment of the problem was issued in September 1961. First, the target to be destroyed was assessed. As the British saw it, three light Russian vehicles were available to be a target; these were the BTR-152, the PT-76 and the BTR-50P. Although little was known of the BTR-50P, it was assessed that armour quality would be about the same hardness, 220bhn, as samples of the BTR-152 that had been studied. The armour was guessed at as roughly 25mm as an upper limit, and this was the benchmark to be defeated by the weapon. One other difference between the United States and UK calculations was the number of casualties needed to be caused. The United States was of the opinion that causing just two casualties to the crew and passengers of the BTR-50P would render the unit incapable of combat operations. The British thought this was unrealistic, suggesting that the Russians were highly-motivated and trained with good morale. To this end, they set the minimum casualties as eight. The other way to render an AFV incapable of combat is to immobilize it. Here again, the United States' and UK criteria were different. The United States required that the vehicle be immobilized within twenty minutes. The UK lowered the time to zero to thirty seconds in the interim report; due to lack of data for the full report they used the United States' criteria, with a note that should the immobilization requirement need to be within thirty seconds, the results should be reassessed.

The original GSOR also included the requirement to be of use against low-performance aerial vehicles. The most common of these would be helicopters, although flying platforms were also considered. This led to some issues as the performance required for use against armoured fighting vehicles and the anti-air requirements seemed to contradict each other with the AA use needing a high rate of fire and large ammunition stocks. A gun with high mechanical accuracy was seen as a negative in the AA role. This last idea might seem odd, and it was questioned by the reader of the report with that claim underlined and question marks noted in the margin. The high accuracy as a negative is due mainly to an inaccurate gun allowing rounds to be spread about a bit and thus stand a higher chance of hitting, or if the burst is well aimed, it spreads the damage around the airframe. In the interim report, many weapons were considered. These included 20mm and 30mm Hispano-Suiza cannons, the former being developed for German use. The Germans had selected their weapon mainly on the choice of what gun they had been using before. There was also a hypothetical 20mm or 30mm self-loading gun, with a single shot or five-round bursts, the latter for AA use. Other weapons included a 20mm Vulcan gun, with a magazine of either 750 or 1,000 rounds, and a mysterious weapon listed as the 50mm 'Tankard' recoilless rifle. This weapon was developed in 1946 by DARDE (back then it was known as ARDE). The weapon was some 8ft 4in long and the barrel weighed about 100lb. The calibre was 50mm, and it fired an APDS projectile weighing 1.58lb at 3,800fps. The interim report did suggest that the same weapon could fire a full calibre APHE shell at about 2,800fps as well, although the report's author did point out that the engineers designing tanks had not been approached on how they would mount a recoilless rifle in an armoured vehicle and that it would require quite some work. Due to the AA requirement, the interim report included two weapons solely for AA use; these were racks of twelve 1.5in or 2in rockets and the Redeye Sam.

The summary of the report concludes that the 20mm weapons were generally just too ineffective and lacked the muzzle velocity to achieve the required level of accuracy. While 40mm would be a good choice of calibre, its weight was prohibitive. For that reason, 35mm was seen as the upper limit in weight terms. Equally a 30mm weapon would cut the weight of the gun by about a fifth, yet still be lethal enough and have the performance against ground targets, but would be lacking in the AA role.

It seems odd to be considering the weight of the gun, especially as earlier the British were ignoring the weight requirements for being dismounted, unlike the US. However, as we will see, the AFV in which this gun was to be mounted had weight as a significant consideration. The report concludes with the request for more information.

There were some flies in the ointment, which caused delays in the final report. In September 1961 an order was placed with Rheinmetall (owners of Hispano-Suiza) for modern 20mm ammo of varying types to test the lethality of it and provide the trials requested. After a year, in August 1962, a handful of practice rounds were delivered. Fed up with this, the UK cancelled its order and used the limited data from United States' tests for the VRFWS. The United States had selected the Hispano-Suiza as the interim version of the VRFWS, but only after Hispano-Suiza promised delivery of quantities of ammunition and guns for tests in the US, an order that had not been fulfilled by the time the interim report was produced. It does appear, however, that the order did eventually get filled, as the United States used the M139 20mm gun as its interim VRFWS.

In March 1964 the final report was issued, although by this point GSOR 1012 had been withdrawn due to a reassessment of the previously listed Soviet AFVs used as targets. There had been mention of a new eight-wheeled Soviet APC (the BTR-70) which had shown that the armour protection ascribed to them in the GSOR was overly generous. However, as it was considered likely that armour values of that thickness could theoretically be seen, the work had continued. The report cited that the Germans were fitting their new AFV with 30mm armour and that was viewed as the benchmark. The removal of the GSOR also removed the problem of the AA requirement, which eliminated the need to mount a complicated fire control system or two weapons.

The final report considered the following guns: L60 and L70 Bofors guns, an L5 76mm gun and a 40/30 Littlejohn gun. The last weapon fired a 30mm tungsten projectile, which was fired at varying velocities to determine the critical velocity. To defeat 30mm sloped at 60 degrees it needed a muzzle velocity of 3,200fps. However, lethality from fragmentation was seen as inadequate, especially at lower armour thicknesses: 10mm plate only produced a few fragments in a cone with a semi-angle of 10 degrees. Against 30mm plate adequate fragmentation was caused by a cone of about 15 degrees semi-angle. In one trial an armour plate was placed to simulate the opposite wall of an AFV's fighting compartment. Upon impact the tungsten core failed to over-penetrate and shattered, producing significant fragmentation. The tests also included various 20mm, 30mm and 35mm cannons from Hispano-Suiza and Oerlikon, although there were problems with obtaining enough ammunition for the tests and some of the rounds were losing their driving bands during the tests. Several types of ammunition were tried including API, HEAT and practice. These were fired at varying muzzle velocities. The Oerlikon rounds were judged to be slightly more lethal due to them being filled with a small amount of high explosive.

Of all the tests the 76mm HESH round produced the best lethality; in both the 10mm and 20mm plate tests the HESH round penetrated the armour before detonating, ripping the plate apart. Against the 30mm target, a 6in scab was blasted off the inside, leaving a 3in hole and a considerable amount of fragmentation. These results were confirmed by tests against a Daimler armoured car in 1962. The problem, however, was accuracy. The gun needed to knock out a single target every ten seconds at 1,000 metres. A 76mm gun did not have that ability to range and successfully hit quickly enough. Equally the report calculated the weight of ammo needed to knock out a target, considering all types of ammo at various muzzle velocities. Again, the best compromise of all the factors was the self-loading 30mm. This idea was developed into the 30mm RARDEN gun, a weapon that has served the British army for decades.

To summarize the British view, they felt that a 30mm semi-automatic firing an APHE-style shell at 3,400fps would provide the best weapon, able to kill enemy light armour at 1,000m. Thus RARDE began working on the design, under the name Project 1186. From the start, it was to be a forward-ejecting weapon loaded with clips containing six rounds, which it could fire in a burst function or single shot. The burst function was dropped quite early on in the weapon's life, possibly to coincide with the loss of the AA requirement. Developed by RARDE and the Royal Small Arms Factory (RSAF), Enfield it was given the name RARDEN, after RARDE and the 'EN' from Enfield, the earliest document suggesting that the name was dated 29 March 1967. Throughout its early life, it was considered for alternative platforms such as replacing the Royal Navy's ageing 20mm and 40mm guns, for fitting to helicopters and hovercraft. In all of these roles, the lack of automatic fire would have been a big negative. The RARDEN was also hoped to achieve export successes by promoting it for the secondary armament of the new MBT-70 being developed by Germany and the United States, which was likely a false hope as both nations had their own cannon armament to use.

While the studies into the ideal weaponry were under way, the vehicle on which to mount it was undergoing some revision. A large number of designs to meet the relevant GSORs for the reconnaissance vehicle APRV and APAFV were submitted to the General Staff on 7 December 1961. These contained both wheeled and tracked schemes. Due to the similarities in all the designs, the requirements were merged. A working party under Major General James d'Avigdor-Goldsmid, who had taken over as DRAC from Major General Hopkinson in October, was set up. Once this working group had finished, the General Staff re-wrote GSOR 1010 to cover all light AFVs for the future period. The revised GSOR 1010 was issued in January 1963 and called for a reconnaissance vehicle, named Armoured Vehicle Reconnaissance (AVR) and a vehicle based upon the AVR but more heavily armed, which was known as the fire support version. A study was authorized on 23 January 1963, and the FVRDE started work on the problem, issuing its final report in December of that year. During the work, an interesting problem cropped up. The GSOR could not contain enough information on the intended use of the equipment. This led to the possibility that certain research and development avenues would be closed off. The fear was that halting research into these ideas would prevent studies that would have created useful equipment. To that end, a series of informal meetings was held between the DRAC, the FVDRE and the subordinate design branches. These allowed the DRAC to explain the thinking behind the requirements in far greater detail than would usually be available and was cited as being invaluable to the design study.

The first design to fulfil GSOR 1010, later named Scheme A, was limited by a weight of 15 tons. This was due to the need to drop the vehicle in full battle trim, i.e. fully loaded with ammo and fuel. This cut into the base weight of the vehicle. In addition, the FVRDE imposed a penalty to the weight to allow spare capacity for the vehicle to gain weight during its development, as frequently happens.

The vehicle was a 6x6 wheeled armoured car. Each of the 14x30 wheels was powered, with the fore and rear pairs being steerable. The tyres were ten-ply thickness conventional rubber designs. These could be switched out for run-flats under certain conditions. Run-flat tyres were not fitted as standard due to speed issues. If the run-flats were driven at over 45mph, they would overheat and fail. As the vehicle could do 54mph in either direction, this was a real issue. The suspension was of torsion bar type and included 16in of movement. The monocoque hull was made of steel armour; the armour was of uniform thickness, but all angled to give the required immunity to enemy fire. With a few minor modifications to the angles of the plates, the material could be changed to a light alloy. These changes were as small as 1 or 2 degrees. The immunity levels needed were to be proof against 14.5mm at 600m, and 12.7mm at 100m through the frontal 90 degrees. Sides were to be proof against .30 Browning machine-gun AP, which was estimated to be about the same performance as the Russian 7.62mm rounds. Everywhere else was to be proof against 105mm shrapnel from a burst at a range of 90ft. Due to the sloping, the minimum thickness was for a 0-degree strike from the 105mm shrapnel; this required a 12mm thick plate.

The engine, mounted in the rear of the vehicle, proved a bit of a problem. Rolls-Royce were contracted to the FVRDE to conduct research on light engines. The requirement asked for levels of mobility to be the same or better than the Ferret. The engine was required to be multi-fuel, which was obviously attractive to war planners expecting a nuclear battlefield. However, as would soon be shown in the Chieftain, reliable multi-fuel engines were horribly hard to produce. To achieve the required degree of performance, it needed to produce 378hp. At the time there were no engines that fitted that requirement available within the size. The closest that could be found was, by a curious coincidence, a Rolls-Royce K60 engine equipped with a turbocharger, which was under development. That would provide 80 per cent of the requirement, with 300hp. Rolls-Royce were confident that they could further develop the engine up to 350hp.

There was an alternative engine suggested. At the time the United States was of the opinion that the M551 Sheridan would fulfil the British requirement and were pushing for the UK to buy that design. As we saw earlier, however, the main armament on the tank was not liked by the British. The GMC 6V53T engine, however, while not multi-fuel, was smaller and would fit in the engine bay. As the engine was smaller, it could mean a shorter chassis, saving some 500lb of weight. It would also allow the fitting of a flexible coupling. The engine was also cheaper on a per unit basis and provided even easier maintenance. Against it were the fact that the 300hp output was about the upper limit of the development of the engine, and it would mean adding an entirely new engine and the logistics burden, which would drive up the cost. There was one further engine suggestion: to fit a gas turbine. Such an engine would fit into the engine compartment built for the K.60. This engine was suggested as a future upgrade as it was estimated it would take about seven years of work and £2 million in development costs. For those reasons, the designers stuck with the Rolls-Royce offering.

The turret was mounted slightly forward of the middle of the vehicle on a 63in turret ring, and was made of 45-degree plates to provide the maximum internal storage. The main gun in the turret, with an elevation of +30 to –10 degrees, was not to be the RARDEN. Because at this point the gun had not been selected or designed, the standard fallback was the 76mm gun, which was to be a copy of the L5 76mm gun as mounted in a Saladin, only constructed of lightweight alloys. This semi-automatic gun was due to fire several types of shell. First among them was an improved general-purpose round. This dual-purpose (DP) shell was a HESH round, which gives anti-tank and HE effects. It was to be redesigned from the round used in the Saladin as improved ballistics and lethality were desired over the predecessor. This improved HESH round was also to provide the basis for a smoke round. In addition, the gun could fire illumination and canister rounds. It was suggested to give a very limited AA deterrent by firing the canister round in the general direction of the target aircraft, which by the sounds of it even the author of the report felt was more vain hope than an actual threat. Mounted coaxially to the main gun was the British army's standard general-purpose machine gun (GPMG); at first, it thought to use this to range the main gun to give better long-range accuracy from the 76mm HESH. However, trials had shown that if the gun was hot from firing and the barrel in less than good condition, accuracy suffered. To that end, it was proposed to mount either the .50 spotting rifle taken from the 120mm WOMBAT recoilless rifle or the .50 ranging machine gun from the Chieftain tank. A third option was to install a second GPMG, and use the second one only for ranging, which should keep the barrel wear down and the gun cool enough to work. The gunner was to the right-hand side of the main gun, with the loader in the rear of the turret. Curiously, the commander was to the left-hand side of the gun. This position was chosen to move

Artist's impression of the GSOR 1010 scheme A1.

the commander's cupola forward to clear the launch envelope of the Swingfire missiles (see Chapter 14). The requirements called for the AVR to have four Swingfire missiles and the support version to have ten. At first, there was an idea to mount the missiles externally, but this was rejected out of hand by the army due to the missiles being exposed to enemy action. Therefore at least some of the missiles had to be placed under armour, which leads to the first split in the design, with Schemes A1 and A2 denoting the different versions.

Scheme A1 had four missiles in an armoured box directly behind the commander. These missiles were behind a bulkhead and thus separated from the fighting compartment. Scheme A2 had the four missiles mounted in the front hull, which caused the driver to be moved to the right-hand side of the hull. In both cases, the armoured missile bins had power-operated armoured lids. Like so many things in armour design, these two schemes brought compromises. Scheme A1 was the most straightforward design, both from a technical standpoint and an operating point of view; however, it was heavier. The weight penalty came from having to armour the missiles, while the A2 version used the armour of the hull that was already on the tank. Technical difficulties called for a link between the missile controller, the role of which fell to the commander, and the launchers. As he was mounted in a fully rotating turret, it also created operating difficulties. If on Scheme A2 the turret was traversed outside the missiles' engagement angle and the commander wanted to fire, then it might cause some considerable confusion. The risk of confusion was made even worse on the support version. On both vehicles, the six extra missiles were strapped to the back of the turret. Thus the A2 had six missiles with 360 degrees of arc and four with 90 degrees.

This problem of arcs was not actually the biggest problem facing the GSOR 1010. The weight of the vehicle was spiralling upwards. Even the most conservative estimates, with the best possible numbers, were showing a vehicle over the target weight. For that reason, work began on Scheme B, which built on a feature of the AVR: its reverse driving ability. In Scheme A the reverse steering was done by the commander who would have control over the accelerator and steering from his cupola, while the driver had control of the gears and brakes. The idea behind Scheme B was to remove the driver entirely and give full controls to the turret. This arrangement, it was calculated, would only save about 600lb and have the disadvantage of making the vehicle vastly more mechanically complicated, as well as overwhelming the crew.

For those reasons Scheme B was dropped and Scheme C was started; this again brought out the three-man crew and gave the AVR a diet of epic proportions. The working idea behind the vehicle was to remove the turret and one of the crew. Neither of these options was liked by the RAC; however, the low silhouette was much appreciated. To the top of the roof, the tank was about 6ft tall; a whole foot lower than Scheme A. The main

Artist's impression of the GSOR 1010 scheme C.

body of the vehicle consisted of 45-degree plates running up to the top of the mudguards, then angling back in at 45 degrees to the roof. At the front hull right up against the lower front plate were five Swingfire missiles, stored under armour. Behind this, about halfway up the upper front hull was the main gun in a traversable mount that was able to swing the gun through 40 degrees either side. The elevation was the same as Scheme A. To the rear of the gun breech, on the left-hand side of the vehicle, sat the driver, who doubled as the loader. Parallel to him was the gunner. Behind both of them in the middle of the vehicle sat the commander with a cupola mounting a GPMG and the Swingfire sight; this had a full 360-degree traverse. Thirty-five rounds of 76mm were carried: thirteen ready, fifteen fighting and seven replenishments. The reverse driving controls were mounted directly onto the firewall for the commander to use. The support version had nine Swingfires, and the extra four were mounted recessed into the mudguards.

All schemes were due to be fully amphibious with a pair of water jets mounted for propulsion. To achieve flotation several options were considered. Foam-filled tanks on the tank increased width and bulk considerably. Inflatable air bladders were vulnerable to enemy fire, and the engine deck needed to be sealed first to avoid flooding the engine. The solution was the tried and tested DD screen, which added about 4in to the width of the vehicle. Technology had moved on a bit though with the development of the 'pram hood', which was a subsection on the upper part of the screen. It was attached to the main armament, which was then fully elevated, raising the hood. With the hood raised, it allowed the vehicle to enter the water from up to a 24-degree slope. Once in the water, the gun could be depressed, which lowered the hood and gave an opening through which the main gun could be fired, or even Swingfires launched, albeit through a limited arc and with no more than 0 degrees gun depression. This hood was not available on Scheme C.

Each vehicle was also to be fitted with a range of equipment as standard. This included a ground surveillance radar with a range of 5,000m, although on the support versions the radar was removed and more ammunition was stowed. An infrared vision device was also standard for all crew bar the loader; one source even says this was a passive system. Other equipment included radiological survey equipment, a navigation aid system, and overpressure chemical and biological protection systems, which would also pipe filtered air to each crew station so they could plug their respirators into it. This plethora of electrical equipment caused some problems with electrical supply, especially during silent watch periods. To this end three sets of batteries were installed, each set consisting of a pair of two 91lb 1ft square batteries. One was to be isolated and used only for automotive requirements such as starting the engine. One was to run the radios; the final set was to provide power for all the other equipment. This collection of hardware and ideas would have made the GSOR 1010 vehicle one of the most technologically-advanced variants of the time, and technology costs money.

It will be no surprise that in early 1964 GSOR 1010 was reviewed, and concerns over the cost were raised. Other descriptions of it included bulky, too heavy and too complicated. The need for AVR, however, still had not diminished. So, for a second time, the GSOR was re-written into a new requirement, this time numbered GSOR 3301. After consultation, the requirements were issued on 10 August 1964. It called for a family of seven vehicles on a standard chassis. These were an anti-APC version mounting the 30mm RARDEN gun; an anti-tank version mounting Swingfire missiles; a support version with a 76mm gun; a liaison vehicle; a command vehicle; an APC and finally an ambulance version.

At about the same time GSOR 3038 was created, which called for a Light High Mobility Tracked Vehicle (LHMTV) family. As there was a significant lack of manpower and resources to do both jobs, the study limited itself to vehicles that could fulfil both GSORs.

The same department of the FVRDE that undertook the previous study was given the task of conducting this one. This decision had the advantage of drawing on a lot of the previous work. This time around the design was fully tracked. The requirements laid down some detailed numbers, such as needing 5kn in water and the ability for the crew to live in and operate the tank, fully closed down, for twenty-four hours. The requirement for air portability was also changed to one that gave a much better chance of success. For transport by air two of these vehicles were required to fit in the back of a Hawker Siddeley HS681 transport. There was also a need to air-drop a single vehicle from the same aircraft. Critically it only had to be droppable carrying 50 per cent of its full load of fuel and ammunition, which would save a significant amount of weight. The air-droppable version was also to be within action within five minutes of landing. The idea behind the AVR was also of interest to the French, and an effort had been made to create a combined requirement that both countries would acknowledge. The French equivalent of GSOR

3301 was Finabel No.13A5. Although both requirements could be met mostly by a standard chassis, it was still divergent on a few critical points, and so the two countries went their separate ways.

The levels of armour protection were identical to GSOR 1010; however, as the entire tank was to be made from a light alloy the plate thickness had to be increased to 28.57mm. There was one exception to the use of light alloy: the air intake louvres were to be of steel; the reason behind this was that using light alloy would be an 'embarrassment'. There was also an increase in the protection required; it was desired to protect against 20mm cannon fire over the frontal 60-degree arc. This requirement was solved by the idea of fitting 40mm appliqué that could be transported separately. Protection against guided anti-tank weapons was also desired; however, the study notes that no such system currently existed. This statement is an odd claim because in 1961 there were preliminary trials on how to defeat guided warheads, and a brief summary of these was presented at the RAC conference of that year. One option for protection hints at explosive reactive armour. The other two defences exploit the long flight time of the missile. The first was the idea of shooting down the missile and the British had achieved such a feat, but to the minds of the scientists, the problems of slewing a gun on to an approaching missile were too great. The other defence, which was in its early stages of development, was to lay a blob of smoke some 200 yards from the tank, which would cause the missile to lose guidance and thereby miss the tank. This principle had been tested against a Vigilant missile and found to work.

The AVR only weighed some 6.75 tons; this was because of the requirement for mobility that had been laid down in GSOR 1010 and expanded further in 3301. One change was the need for the vehicle to operate in difficult terrain as found in bushfire wars. This requirement is as close as any document seen by the author comes to the myth about the FV101 Scorpion being designed to fit between trees on a Malayan rubber plantation track. To meet the requirements, engines with only an output of 200hp were needed. This output would be able to propel the tank between 2 and 45mph, although it was hoped to achieve 50mph. Again, there was a lack of multi-fuel engines in this size and weight range with that level of output. This time the designers selected two engines for use: these were the Daimler D2458, giving 220hp, and the Rolls-Royce F60, with a current output of 160hp but being developed to produce 200hp. As before, a gas turbine was suggested as a viable option in the future;

one proposed model was from the Rover Gas Turbine Co. At the time there was no experience of a gas turbine fitted to an armoured vehicle, so it was decided not to follow the idea at this time. When travelling cross-country, AVR could manage a 2-metre-wide trench and a step of 90cm. For gradients, the tracked solution was calculated as being able to handle a 60 per cent slope and could stop and start on a 45 per cent slope.

The suspension, which was bolted directly to two longitudinal beams to form the chassis, was of a hydro-pneumatic type. This arrangement allowed the AVR to adjust its suspension, and tilt its body for extra gun elevation; this, in turn, allowed the trunnion height to be reduced. The suspension could also be firmed up to provide a more stable firing platform. Finally, it allowed the idler wheel to be lowered to the ground, and this reduced the AVR's 5lb/in^2 ground pressure by a further 30 per cent.

The tracks were also made of light alloy and had rubber pads. The wheel path was recessed into the tracks to prevent track throwing. The tracks would provide a speed of 5kn in the water. The tank itself was naturally buoyant, but only had 5in of freeboard. For that reason, it needed a wave screen fitting to prevent it from being swamped.

All three of the combat versions – the anti-APC, the anti-tank and the fire support – had an identical hull, with only the turrets needing to be changed to alter their role. Consequently, they also had the same 57in turret ring. They also all had three crew. The driver was located

Artist's impression of the GSOR 3301 fire support.

at the front of the tank on the left-hand side sitting beside the engine compartment. In the anti-APC and fire support versions, the commander doubled as the gunner. In the fire support version, he was placed to the front right of the turret, while the loader was to the rear left. The loader, who also doubled as the radio operator, had a foldable seat to ride on. When in action he would kneel on the turret floor so that he could access 76mm ammo racks in the back of the fighting compartment. These racks held forty rounds, seventeen of which were ready, the rest were fighting rounds. No ranging machine gun was fitted to save weight, but the fire support version did mount a GPMG beside its main gun.

On the anti-APC version, the commander sat at the middle rear of the turret, with the gun on the left of the turret and the coaxial machine gun on the right. The loader sat, rotated through about 240 degrees from the front of the tank, beneath the coaxial machine gun. It seems perplexing to place a loader for a RARDEN gun in such a position. However, it should be remembered at this stage that the gun that would be developed into the RARDEN gun had not been entirely designed. During this period the gun was seen as being loaded with five-round clips that could be fired either in single shot or a burst of all five rounds. Thus, loading would be more akin to fitting a magazine to an assault rifle or submachine gun, which makes the placement of the loader seem far more logical. The loader did have his own escape hatch, only it was built into the turret side and not the roof.

In the last of the GSOR 3301 trio, the anti-tank version, the turret has the gunner to the front, slightly offset to the left, while the commander is directly behind him, slightly offset to the right. To the gunner's right and the commander's front right is the single GPMG. On either side of this

Artist's impression of the GSOR 3301 anti-APC.

Artist's impression of the GSOR 3301 anti-tank.

turret are armoured racks of Swingfire missiles, containing the vehicle's entire complement of six missiles. All are under armour with hinged lids. When ready to fire, the missiles elevate from their carry position. The turret has a full 360-degree traverse.

The ancillary vehicles were all very similar and looked like an AVR hull without a turret. The APC could carry four men, as well as the driver, plus equipment and stores for them. The ambulance could carry two stretchers, although by smart design it was suggested that more could be fitted, or four seated wounded. To fulfil GSOR 3038, the common chassis in the shape of the hull, engine running gear and driver's position was utilized. The rear of the tank that would normally mount the turret was fitted for different uses. The most comprehensive re-work was the close-support weapon system. The name does imply something like the Second World War idea of a close-support tank firing smoke, which is misleading. It was a self-propelled artillery piece. The gun was given as a '105mm light gun'. One suspects that

Above and below: Sketch of the close-support artillery system, showing the gun in its stowed position and with the roof slid backwards to provide a covered workspace while its crew are manning the gun.

this was a very early concept for the L118 105mm Light Gun that was starting its design and development life at about the same time. Indeed, the diagrams bear more than a passing resemblance to the L118. During transport, the gun would be stowed traversed all the way to the right and locked into position. The vehicle had space for three passengers seated facing right along the left-hand side of the hull immediately behind the driver. One would guess that the driver would also be part of the gun detachment.

The gun mount was in the centre rear of the vehicle, to the third passenger's right. When the gun was to be brought into action the driver's part of the front hull would fold down, allowing the gun full traverse. Then the roof and upper sides of the superstructure slid backwards, freeing the gun to be elevated and provide cover against enemy shrapnel to the gun detachment as the piece was operated. The gun vehicle did not carry any ammunition, but it could tow a limber. In addition, the limber was to be made of components from the normal L118's carriage. Such a set-up would allow the gun to be dismounted from its chassis and transferred to the limber to create a towed version of the light gun. Another option was to have a second vehicle to act as an ammunition carrier. Also, this allowed the 105mm to be dismounted and moved to the second vehicle if the first became somehow disabled. The arc for the gun in action was 30 degrees to either side and an elevation of 0-70 degrees. The hydro-pneumatic suspension allowed the tank to change the angle of its hull; this allowed the gun to depress to –6 degrees.

The GSOR 3038 also called for the APC version to be able to carry either an 81mm mortar or an L6 120mm WOMBAT recoilless rifle in a portée style. The WOMBAT was simply winched into position and could be fired from the vehicle with a –10 to +17-degree elevation. The 81mm mortar had its base plate built into the rear door, and its tube lying

Artist's impression of the GSOR 3038 Wombat Portée.

118

Artist's impression of the GSOR 3038 Swingfire carrier.

A sketch of the GSOR 3038 anti-tank; in this picture it can be seen that the launchers can be raised or lowered in stacks of three. It also shows off the armoured box at the back where the commander and gunner would sit. Considering the problems encountered with the Swingfire and using forward efflux, one wonders about the practicality of such an arrangement.

119

Artist's impression of the GSOR 3038 convoy escort.

parallel to the floor. The door would fold down, bringing the mortar into action almost immediately.

The anti-tank version of GSOR 3038 had twelve Swingfires fitted in a square frame, which was surrounded by an armoured box. The structure lay flat while travelling but would elevate for firing. The commander and gunner were in an armoured box behind the frame at the rear of the vehicle.

The final GSOR 3038 vehicle that was fully worked up under GSOR 3301 was a light vehicle for convoy escort and internal security duties. It was armed with a 20mm cannon and a GPMG in a small rounded turret. The crew consisted of a driver plus a single man in the turret. The 20mm cannon was selected as it did not require a loader and was ideal for deterring, if not actually being able to shoot down aircraft. Equally the gun would be useful against infantry. It was suggested that should the insurgents be in dense woods, that the cannon should be fired into the treetops to get a sort of airburst effect. This idea was backed up by citing German actions in the Second World War when the same thing was done against Soviet partisans.

There were two GSOR 3038 vehicles that fell outside the scope of GSOR 3301 due to weight. These were a tank destroyer version and a self-propelled rocket-launching system. The former was armed with a 120mm recoilless rifle in a turret. Although the turret could traverse a

A sketch showing the GSOR 3038 Tank Destroyer, with its 120mm recoilless rifle ready to fire.

full 360 degrees, the arc of fire was limited to 270 lest the blast from the Venturi damaged the front of the tank. The tank itself carried ten rounds of ammunition with a simple loading assist mechanism. After firing the gun would slide forward, leaving the Venturi in place at the rear of the turret. Moving the barrel like this would open the breech to allow for a new round to be loaded, and then the barrel would slide back into battery.

The other version was the APC chassis fitted with a rack of eight 4.2in rockets, which could traverse through 180 degrees. The vehicle itself would carry ten spare rockets. There was a variant of this vehicle where the launcher was mounted like a portée, and could be removed from the hull and towed on its own carriage; this was to allow the weapon to be carried underslung by helicopter. Both versions could carry the crew of four, although in action all would dismount.

Now that the main reason for the study was finished, the team at the FVRDE did not stop. They started looking at wheeled versions of the AVR. The idea was to see if they could be arranged to meet the air-portability requirements of the GSOR. The original suggestion had failed on the requirements because of weight. The first was called Scheme A. In this the turrets were the same as the regular AVR, and fulfilled the same roles. Scheme A was an armoured car. The hull, with

Above and below: Sketches showing both of the GSOR 3038 multiple rocket-launcher systems. The top one is the complete unit, with the launcher permanently mounted on its hull; the bottom one is the portée version, which would allow the launcher to be dismounted from the vehicle for flexibility and mobility.

its 6x6 wheel arrangement, resembled a sleeker Saladin. This reduction in length was due to the engine being mounted sideways, and that meant that it had to go in the back of the vehicle as it could not fit in beside the driver. The tyres were lightweight run-flat types or sand tyres in some circumstances. Rubber tracks could be fitted over the wheels if needed. The tyres could have the inflation pressure controlled by the driver. Steering was done by skid-steer manoeuvre, and the vehicle could get up to 55mph. Although this meant fitting the same 240hp engine as the Scheme A designs, it made the complete vehicle heavier, weighing in at about 8 tons. The wheels did reduce its cross-country ability as it could only handle a 1.5-metre trench and a step of 50cm.

Due to this weight and the potential cost implications, it was decided to offer a solution that showed what could be done by cutting the weight as much as possible. This group of vehicles was named Scheme B. This was AVR on an extreme diet, with the radar, filtered air and night sights stripped out. Also removed was the water propulsion. Now the wheels had to be used and would be able to propel the vehicle at 2 to 3kn. The crew compartment was also smaller and the fuel capacity reduced by

Artist's impression of the GSOR 3301 Scheme B.

10 gallons. Overall Scheme B was also smaller. It had a 50in turret ring, and the overall dimensions were the same as the Ferret, apart from in height, where Scheme B was just 5in taller. When compared to Scheme A the difference was a whole 12in of length and width, and 9in in height. This whole exercise also imposed the obvious penalty of less crew space and an even further reduced trench-crossing ability, with Scheme B only managing 1.2 metres. The weight loss also meant that smaller wheels and a lighter clutch could be used. The result was saving some 3,000lb in weight, which resulted in an even higher power to rate ratio and a speed of 65mph.

There was also a Scheme C, which was for the ancillary vehicles of the GSOR 3301. These wheeled vehicles had their width increased to 8ft, but seemingly very little was done with them due to the apparent shortcomings of the wheeled solutions. These problems were not only weight-based; Scheme B weighed roughly the same as the tracked AVR solution but had less mobility. A test vehicle called the TV1000 was built. This used 6x6 skid-steering very similar to the planned fit on the Scheme A. It was tested in a variety of soils and roles; one showed a loss of steering authority when used in wet ploughed peaty soil, much like most of the terrain of northern Germany. Considering that the expected theatre of operations was most likely Germany, this was probably the final nail in the wheeled vehicle's coffin.

Cost estimates were of course needed for the Treasury development budget. It was estimated to cost £5.6 million and take between eight and eight and a half years. This development plan would involve the production of twenty-eight prototypes. These included a hull shell and fire-support turret shell for firing trials. There was also one each of the anti-tank and anti-APC turret shells for firing tests as well. Oddly both of the latter also had complete turrets listed for shooting at, yet the fire-support version did not have an entire turret or hull listed for resistance evaluation.

The study into GSOR 3301 was completed at a critical time. The Canadians were working on their CL91 Dynatrac vehicle, which was seen as a competitor. Equally, the Indian government had made enquiries of Vickers to look at a tracked reconnaissance vehicle. Also, Australia had asked the United States for such a vehicle. The United States had been pushing the M551 Sheridan for both the UK and Australian markets. However, the tank was too big for the Commonwealth transport aircraft, and cost about £8,000 per tank and the armament was considered wholly unsuitable. Into this landscape, the AVR emerged.

Although twenty-eight prototypes had been forecast, in the end only one and a half were built. From the stage where the plans were drawn for the AVR, it became known as the TV15000. In keeping with the theme of a switchable turret, a single complete hull was built, which was completed on Christmas Eve 1965. This vehicle was known as the Mobile Test Rig (MTR). As well as the MTR, a partial hull, consisting of just the engine bay and hull structure connected to it, was built to test the vehicle's cooling performance. Originally the MTR was fitted with the hydro-pneumatic suspension, but she was also tested with more conventional torsion bars suspension. The fittings for the suspension were designed to be able to be changed. It was found that the hydro-pneumatic suspension only offered increased cost and complexity with no improvement in ride quality. For that reason, the torsion bar suspension was fitted to the production models.

The first engine fitted was the Rolls-Royce FB60 engine, the same engine as fitted to the BMC Vanden-Plas Princess car. The car theme continued in the choice of a second engine to be installed, which was a 4.2L Jaguar petrol engine; this would be the first engine fitted to the production tanks. This vehicle received the official designation of FV101 Scorpion, which was the parent of the Combat Vehicle Reconnaissance Tracked (CVRT) family. The speed of the tank was emphasized when, in a promotional film, she was raced against a Jaguar sports car. Scorpion would be Britain's last tank design that achieved multiple overseas sales, being purchased by more than twenty countries.

Scheme B, although it failed initially, may have had some bearing on later developments as well. It resembles quite strongly nothing so much as a 6x6 version of the FV721 Fox. Its resemblance is more than likely more than just chance. General Staff Requirement (by now the 'Operational' had been dropped) 3358 was issued in July 1965 and called for a Combat Vehicle Reconnaissance (Wheeled), which would eventually become the FV721 Fox. The FV722 Liaison vehicle, also known as Vixen, fell under GSR 3340. Interestingly, at least in the first instance, the Fox was deemed to be only for colonial policing, and not for use in Europe against the Russians. Fox was designed by the FVRDE, and so it is likely that a lot of the experience of the AVR designs for GSOR 3301 was re-employed in developing Fox.

PART 3

Infantry Armour

Chapter 11

The Smallest Enigma

One of the oddities that marked out the British army of the Second World War was the use of carriers. These started off life as the Carden Loyd machine-gun carriers and progressed through the Vickers D.50. This vehicle, in turn, led to the Cavalry, Machine-Gun, Scout and Bren Gun carriers, the latter being the most common at the start of the war and lending its name to the entire class. All these roles were then combined into the Universal Carrier. This version was so widely used that it became the most-produced armoured vehicle in history with about 113,000 units built. For the majority of the war, this tiny vehicle served as the main type of armour used by the British infantryman, although towards the end of the Second World War there were designs for improvised Armoured Personnel Carriers (APCs) in the form of the Kangaroo. As the war progressed, the British started to look at a successor to the Universal Carrier. The development of these small carriers is one of the biggest mysteries of the dark age. Almost no documents seem to survive in the usual archives. What little remains hints at a tantalizing story of continuous developments that might have far-reaching effects.

These vehicles were identified by the designation CT, which stood for 'carrier, tracked'. The first of the family that is in sequence, although it may not have been the first such vehicle, was the CT20, which later on would become known as the Oxford carrier. Unlike the earlier Universal Carrier, the Oxford had a large crew compartment at the front of the vehicle, with a sloped front. The engine bay was at the rear, and it was liberally covered with storage bins. These were normally for carrying ammunition, as the principal role of the Oxford was as a gun tow. It is in this role that the Oxford became the last carrier to see action with the British armed forces when some Oxfords saw service in the Korean War.

CT21, CT22 or CT23 we have no record of; however, we have a single document on CT24. It was developed by Rolls-Royce, with its

An Oxford carrier with an armoured superstructure fitted. These appear to be fixed on this vehicle, but would be roughly similar in appearance to the folding screens on the Cambridge, once they had been erected.

first historical footprint in March 1945. This particular carrier was designed for the close-support role; thus it was fairly heavily armoured for its size and class. Its frontal armour was 20mm thick, sloped at 41.5 degrees, giving a basis of about 30mm. The floor and sides of the crew compartment were 14mm. While 14mm also protected the engine compartment sides, the floor was just 8mm. Tracks and suspension were of the same sort as previous carrier designs. Overall this vehicle weighed around 6 to 7 tons. In shape, the CT24 looked identical to the Oxford and may have been an attempt to produce a better-protected version of the Oxford for more aggressive use.

Rolls-Royce contacted the DTD and asked them to take the prototype and subject it to trials to test the protection it offered. To this end on 1 March 1945 the prototype was wheeled out onto a range. Originally Rolls-Royce had asked that the vehicle be subjected to Tellermine attack, but it seems the DTD decided as they had the prototype they might as well test out some other forms of attack. The frontal armour was fired at with a 15mm BESA machine gun. These rounds penetrated the armour, then the gun malfunctioned and trials had to be halted.

A lightly-armoured IT130 plate protected the final drive. These and the 14mm sides were subjected to .303 AP shots and resisted them. After these trials, the vehicle was subjected to the mine attack.

As it was missing its tracks, it was ballasted up to the correct weight. Two dummies were placed in it to represent crewmen. In addition, four rabbits in cages were situated in the vehicle: one on each dummy's lap and one under their seats.

A first Tellermine was exploded under the front of the track, where one would logically assume it would explode if the vehicle ran over it. The CT24 was thrown some 18ft, turned through 90 degrees and landed on its side. Worse, the floor bulged inwards and the welds along the bottom of the hull ruptured. After the vehicle was retrieved, a second mine was then detonated under the rear tracks, with similar results.

Although the 14mm floor armour held under the crew compartment, the displacement of the floor was the cause of the majority of the injuries suffered by the rabbits. The 8mm armour under the engine bay failed to withstand the blast. It was found that the welds of the hull had failed as they were undersized to that specified and so deemed substandard.

The Rolls-Royce CT24 close-support carrier, without tracks or any of the attachments on the ranges before it was shot at and blown up. The hull shape is similar to that used on the Oxford and Cambridge, only on those vehicles the shape is obscured by stowage boxes.

From then on the CT24 disappears. Shortly afterwards the Oxford entered service around 1946.

It seems that the Oxford was fated to serve as a testing platform in support of the development of the FV400, which was designated CT25 and gained the name Cambridge. The War Office was looking at the FV400 from shortly after the war. In June 1947 an Oxford was used for loading trials to see if a Cambridge could fit inside a Hamilcar glider. The trial was carried out at Lasham airfield, and the glider was flown with the carrier inside. It was found that the Oxford had just 1in clearance in height and that a tin can had to be placed over the exhaust to prevent it from causing damage to the rear wall; this included setting the wooden glider alight, a particular hazard as no fire extinguisher was carried. The Oxford used 12in-wide tracks, and a normal Cambridge had 18in tracks. Because of this increase, special 10.5in tracks had been developed for the Cambridge to enable it to be used by airborne forces, but even these would not allow the Cambridge to be fitted into the glider as the vehicle was 3in higher and 9in longer than a Hamilcar's cargo bay. The main reason for this increase in dimensions was the change to torsion bar suspension.

Here we see an Oxford being unloaded from a Hamilcar glider. It can instantly be seen what a tight squeeze it was to get the vehicle inside the load bay.

Otherwise, the two vehicles looked identical, again hinting at a continuous line of development. WOPS 26 had originally laid out the requirements for the carrier. It was to provide the roles of infantry carrier, 3in mortar carrier, Medium Machine-Gun carrier, and to be used as a tow for both normal anti-tank guns and the new recoilless rifle anti-tank weapons, with the 3in and medium machine gun being fired from under cover of the armour.

In 1947, before the FV401 had even been designed, it was decided that the carrier would also mount a flame-thrower so that it could replace the Wasp currently in service. This flame-thrower was envisioned to be along the same lines as Red Cyclops. The equipment was code-named Red Achilles. The flame gun was similar to the tank-mounted weapon but was limited to 6 gallons per second. Control was to be by hand rather than by hydraulic pressure. Range was also reduced to a minimum of 150 yards, and a desired 200 yards. The fuel was fed from two cylindrical 50-gallon tanks, with a piston at each end. A number of propulsion systems were considered; first were cordite charges being used to create gas pressure directly propelling the pistons. An alternative to this was reduced gas pressure to discharge a container

The soldier standing in this Cambridge carrier has just grasped the edge of the forward screen and is about to raise it up. The main way to identify a Cambridge or an Oxford is to look at the suspension. If it has Horstmann-type suspension, similar to that used on a Universal Carrier from the Second World War, it is an Oxford. The Cambridge has no visible suspension, just four large wheels.

into a propulsion unit, much the same way in which the Red Cyclops worked. The designs for the propulsion unit fell into two types: either a rotary pump driven by an engine or even a gas turbine or an accumulator and reciprocating pump driven by cordite charges. Red Achilles, like her larger sisters, was cancelled before the Cambridge came into being.

WOPS26 called for a high level of performance from the Cambridge. She was fitted with a Rolls-Royce B80 Mk 5F engine, which propelled the carrier at 35mph, a speed she could reach in 36.4 seconds from a standing start. The trials also had the carrier climbing a 505-yard course on Beacon Hill in Dorset, which had an average 1:10 gradient. The Cambridge was able to scramble up the slope at a rate of 8ft per second, giving a speed of 20mph. When towing a 17-pounder, the carrier recorded a time of 89.5 seconds, which equated to an average speed of 15mph. In the water, her tracks were able to drive the Cambridge at 2.75kn.

The trials also covered quite some distance, both with and without the 17-pounder tow. When two of the torsion bar suspension elements failed, they had each covered at least 5,600 miles, with the third prototype being run to 6,163 miles in total. There were some defects discovered during these trial runs. There was a very high rate of transfer of oil between the engine and the Hobbs TN21 gearbox. During the cooling trial, there was a transfer of some 5 pints. The average across the tests, even with several attempts by the trials team to fix the problem, was 59.2 miles per pint of oil.

The FV401 had an all-up weight of some 9.5 tons. The weight of the Cambridge was considerably heavier than a Universal Carrier, which was only about 3.5 tons. This weight may have had an impact on later developments and may even have been the missing link between the carriers and the later APCs. A part of the increase was down to the armour. A Universal Carrier only had, at most, 10mm of flat armour. The Cambridge had 8mm of armour, sloped at 41 degrees on her front, which gave a basis of 14mm. Her sides had 12mm, with 6mm pannier boxes and skirts. One curiosity was a series of folding shields that surrounded the fighting compartment. With these down, a Cambridge looked and acted a lot like an Oxford. With them raised they formed a truncated pyramid and carried the slope of the armour upwards, providing additional protection to the crew. These shields were 8mm thick. These plates were sufficient to meet the requirements from the WOPS, which stated that the armour had to protect against .303 AP fired at 200 yards and field artillery and mortar fragments at 40ft. Trials with a 25-pounder and small-arms fire were carried out against the Cambridge on 26 January 1956. This date might give a clue as to what happened to the Cambridge. Initially, it had been slated for production by 31 July 1952. It is likely that project overruns and the changing of the War Office's ideas leading to the FV432 meant that it was cancelled.

To chart the thinking behind the development of the APC, we must go back to the later years of the Second World War. Even before the war had ended, lessons were being studied. One such study was the usefulness of Armoured Personnel Carriers. Up until 1945 the only British experience with APCs was with the aforementioned carriers, or with a handful of Kangaroo APCs in Europe. To that end, around May 1945 the War Office began to consider its policy on APCs and how they would shape the post-war world. A request for views, in the form of a questionnaire, on the APC was issued to both the 8th Army and 21st Army Group. This request was then passed on to all regiments who had used carriers in order to gain their views.

The reviews of the Kangaroos covered the two models that saw service: the RAM and defrocked Priest types. Of the two, the defrocked Priest was seen as the better vehicle as it enabled two sections to be carried in one vehicle, and thus an entire platoon in three vehicles, which was seen as a positive as it kept the number of vehicles involved in the attack down to a minimum. Equally the consensus on the Kangaroo was that it was best as an armoured Troop Carrying Vehicle (TCV). From those reports, it is possible to see that many of these officers saw the APC as nothing more than a glorified truck. The truck connotations were also reinforced by the fact that the officers all thought that the correct organization was for an APC regiment to be part of the Royal Army Service Corps (RASC), although later on a suggestion was made in November 1947 to transfer the APC regiment from the RASC to the RAC. The APCs could be loaned out as needed, like a transport unit made of conventional trucks. The APC regiment could lift a brigade of infantry in a single go. After marrying up the infantry to their transport, the APCs would then drive directly to the dismounting point. Once the infantry had left their vehicles and gone about their business, the APCs would then move to an assembly point. Only one officer, of the 167th London Infantry Brigade, suggested that this idea was wrong. He considered that APCs should be organic to the infantry formation so that the two groups could get to familiarize themselves with each other.

Each officer put forth their perfect APC. Several suggested overhead cover, such as a detachable lightweight armoured screen that could be thrown off to allow easier disembarking. This idea may have led to the shields on the Cambridge. A similar notion suggested a large armoured roller blind. One officer put forth the idea of hatches in the rear or belly to allow troops to disembark under cover.

Armament and battle drills came under particular scrutiny. Nearly all the officers suggested that there was no need for battle drills as the APCs would never use them. Only a few respondents tackled the idea of weaponry. One suggested that a machine gun was useful to suppress enemy *Panzerfaust* detachments. Another suggested that a pair of fixed machine guns fired by the driver would be of value, although how he came to such a conclusion about a concept that had been proved time and again to be of dubious value is not recorded.

One officer, Lieutenant Colonel John Harding, also talked of weapons on his APC, mostly machine guns, as the APC he designed bristled with them. Lieutenant Colonel Harding also helpfully included a sketch of his APC idea with his returned questionnaire. It included smoke dischargers and a machine gun dedicated for AA work as well as several for local defence. One oddity of the design was that the hull sides and the roof

Sketch of his APC design by Lieutenant Colonel Harding. Armed with a bow machine gun and one for AA use, it also carries a smoke grenade-launcher in the roof.

were separated by a small gap, allowing a very good unrestricted view around the APC.

By 1947 the ideas surrounding the issue had coalesced into two vehicles: the Heavy and the Light APC. The heavy is best described by the FV212 mentioned earlier; the light, however, was described as having only about 16mm of armour compared to the 50 to 60mm envisioned for the heavy. It also came with a rear door and a single crewman who was the driver. Of the eleven passengers, one was the vehicle commander and would presumably be the infantry section's commander as well. He would have a cupola armed with a light machine gun. The running gear was to be of the same type as the FV300. From that description, the bare bones of an idea can quite clearly be seen that, when fleshed out, would resemble the FV432. By late 1948 the concept of the Heavy APC had been dropped.

Despite this, it appears that the UK dragged its heels when it came to the Light APC, maybe because it was expecting the FV212 Heavy APC to succeed. It is more likely that this delay was also caused by a need to rethink the role of the APC and move from a separate regiment to lift large numbers of men to an organic vehicle to carry its own section.

In the early 1960s, the situation became so critical that the FV432 was prioritized. To give an idea of how critical the situation was seen to be, the first draft of GSOR 1105 for the FV432 was written in January 1962 and the final acceptance meeting on the same vehicle was in July. This seems like a fast development; however, the FV432 was based upon the FV421 load carrier, which bears a resemblance to the FV400, at least as far as running gear is concerned, and the FV number would indicate a familial link.

In a break with tradition, the development and user trials were run at the same time. Eighteen prototypes were subjected to this brutal series of trials over a five-month period in most corners of the world. The net result was the user trials returning all sorts of horrible defects such as the track pins being too narrow and thus breaking with frightening regularity. By increasing the track pin width from .525in to .625in the problem was solved, and production of the new track began towards the end of 1962. Another defect was that the belly plate kept cracking. This flaw was traced back to the manufacturer who had used the wrong sort of welding which, like the many other defects, was fixed before production.

One of the problems that the FV432 encountered was its name. Originally it was given the name 'Trojan'; however, in December 1962, the solicitors for Trojan Ltd wrote to the MOD complaining that the use of the name was injurious to their clients. Equally the FV431 load carrier was to be called 'Titan'; however, it was advised that Leyland Motors Ltd had registered that for one of their vehicles. A list of alternative names was drawn up for the FV432. These were 'Thruster', 'Tomahawk', 'Tuscan' and 'Troy'. In the end, none of these names was selected, and the name Trojan was officially removed from use in early 1963. In support of this, an announcement was made in *The Times* and technical press, although the MOD resisted Trojan Ltd's request that a full statement be made in the House of Commons.

Chapter 12

The Return of the Infantry Tank

At the user acceptance meeting of the FV432, in July 1962 information was presented to the Director of Infantry (DINF), Major General P. Gleadell, about the new Russian 14.5mm heavy machine gun. At that time, the weapon was able to penetrate the FV432 at somewhere between 800 to 1,000m. In return, the only weapons available to respond were the battalion anti-tank weapons such as the L6 120mm WOMBAT or a Carl Gustav recoilless rifle, the latter of which could be fired from a mount on the back of the FV432, although the arc was restricted to the sides and rear, and only had an effective range of around 350m. If the FV432 was turned to allow the 'Charlie G' to fire at the Soviets, the range at which the 14.4mm could penetrate increased to about 1,200 to 1,300m. At the time, British intelligence considered that about 6 per cent of the APCs in a Russian Motor Rifle Division and 13 per cent in a tank division mounted this weapon and the percentage was expected to rise. The British did consider whether their tanks could solve this issue, but if all the targets were added together, the RAC would be outnumbered about fourteen to one and the tanks would be prioritizing the Russian tanks, as would the heavier infantry anti-tank weapons, leaving the infantry with no weapon to deal with the Soviet light armour. The MOD asked for a brief investigation into the possibility of making the FV432 proof against the 14.5mm at point-blank, 350m and 700m. She was already proof against a Soviet 12.7mm heavy machine gun fired at 200 yards, and the study considered how much the armour would need to be thickened for immunity. The weight penalty turned out to be 1,000lb for immunity at 200m and 500lb at 500m. It was agreed that this increase was unacceptable. Because of this, the DINF suggested that he would need to reconsider the weapons fit on the FV432.

Thus, in July 1963 the DINF issued a GSOR, numbered 3165, for an anti-APC weapon. In addition to the ability to defeat light armour, it was required to have limited anti-air abilities. This weapon was to arm 50 per cent of the APCs in a platoon. The first thoughts were to run to the idea of a pedestal-mounted 20mm HS820. Later the TRW 6425 was considered. The description of the mount as a pedestal is somewhat misleading. Today we would call such a mount a remote weapons station, as it was fired from under armour by remote controls. The cannon was mounted with a fixed amount of ammunition. In the case of the 20mm, this was 350 rounds. The weapon could slew through 360 degrees at the rate of 1 degree per second. Elevation and depression were +90 through to –15 degrees. Aiming was done through a x2.5 or x7 telescope, although there was the suggestion that a x6 would be accepted. The scope was mounted vertically, on the outside of the pedestal; with a tilting prism directly under the weapon this would allow the sight to aim at any location to which the gun could point. Controls were at the base of the pedestal inside the FV432, and any member of the crew could operate it as there was no dedicated position.

During a meeting on 3 June 1964, the requirement was changed to require a full proper turret and the GSR was re-written, which led to the FVRDE undertaking a feasibility study on the subject. The turret

Artist's impression of the FV432 with one-man turret mounting a TRW 6425 cannon.

was required to be fitted to a plate that could be latched onto the mortar hatch on the top of the troop carrier and not protrude into the crew compartment. This later requirement mainly seems to have been applied to traverse gear, meaning that no power traverse could be used.

The FVRDE unsurprisingly chose three weapons for their feasibility study and designed three turrets around them. The choices of weapon were our old friends the HS820, TRW 6425 and the 30mm RARDEN. Of the three, the TRW 6425 caused the most difficulties due to its large size and feed mechanism. The first problem was actually fitting it into a turret. At first, the FVRDE tried fitting the weapon offset to one side with the gunner parallel to the weapon, and so that the gun almost fired over the gunner's right shoulder. The first version had the ammo box behind the gunner's head, but the number of rounds carried was very small. A larger ammo box fit was mounted behind the gun in the next version. However, the external weapons feed and the offset gun meant that the design had to be discarded as it failed to meet the requirements. The next version had the weapon on the centreline and the ammo supply fixed to the gun cradle. In this case, the ammo box was just too massive, to the extent that there was no room for a gunner, and reloading it was almost impossible.

The next version had the gunner directly behind the weapon, with ammo boxes either side of his head. This arrangement had the problems of no room for the coaxial GPMG and inside the turret cartridge ejection, which would cause a toxicity hazard.

Finally, the FVRDE managed to get the weapon to fit by turning it on its side, which allowed them to design the mount so that the cartridge ejection port was in the centre of the trunnion. Such a placement meant that the designers could achieve external ejection by having a step cut into the front profile of the turret. Two ammo boxes were located to the rear of the turret behind the gunner, with feed chutes running around the turret. One box contained sixty-five rounds, the other fifty. The two feed chutes combined would add a further eighty-five rounds total to the load carried.

For the HS820, the same basic design was included, with a step in the frontal armour allowing cases to be ejected through the trunnion. However, the much smaller gun was easier to get inside the turret. One advantage was that the HS820 could carry 200 rounds compared to 170 for the others. There was an alternative design for the HS820, in which

Artist's impression of the FV432 with one-man turret mounting an HS820 20mm cannon.

the entire front of the turret pivoted up and down with the weapon. This mount did provide the advantage of forward ejection, but there were questions about the ability of this to work as the cartridge case had to be deflected in two planes to achieve it.

The final design was the turret mounting the RARDEN. The short inboard length of just 9in and the built-in forward ejection meant that life was straightforward for the designers of the turret.

From a performance point of view, all three turrets were about the same. All had a gun depression of –10 degrees. Elevation ranged from +60 degrees for the TRW 6425, through +65 degrees for the RARDEN, with the HS820 turret having +70 degrees. Armour for the HS820 and TRW 6425 turrets was 18mm at 30 degrees, while the RARDEN turret had 16mm at 36 degrees. The flat front of the RARDEN turret was also seen as providing better projection compared to the turrets with a step in them.

A year later in September 1965 the GSR was downgraded to a General Staff Target (GST) but kept the same number. In April 1966 the RARDEN turret was selected as the best choice. By this point, however, the infantry was getting worried. First, they required the vehicle to

Artist's impression of the FV432 with one-man turret mounting a 30mm RARDEN gun.

keep its carrying capacity the same. Equally, they wanted a seat for the gunner, which would violate the GST stipulation that nothing should protrude below the hull roof. The biggest concern the infantry had was the position of the commander in his traditional place in the hull, and the difficulties it would cause in commanding the section and the turreted gun. Then a final meeting was held on 23 November 1966. The decision had to be taken on which turret to use, in order to meet the in-service deadline. The infantry was told to pick a turret and upgrade to a GSR or go and re-write the GST. The pressure to come to a conclusion was down to the expected life of the turreted FV432. By this point in the late 1960s a dedicated Infantry Fighting Vehicle (IFV) was under consideration; it was called the MICV-80, and was to be built from the ground up as an IFV. It too would mount the RARDEN gun and come into service in the mid-1970s. This date left a very short service window for the turreted FV432, and there was a lot of concern that the turret would come into service just in time to be scrapped, wasting a part of the armed forces' budget.

However, the infantry had come up with a cunning plan. The DINF chose the option to rewrite the GST. Simply they were to ask that an

Artist's impression of the MICV-80. At first glance it looks like an FV510 Warrior; however, this early design has two sub-turrets on the rear roof above the passenger positions. These turrets do not protrude into the fighting compartment and allow two infantrymen to operate the machine guns and provide local defence.

FV721 Fox turret was installed on the FV432. The FVRDE was tasked with undertaking a study, which was completed by March 1967. The study showed that the vehicle would work, and they even managed to keep a carrying capacity of eight men, including the commander who would ride in the turret. The other seven men would be positioned with four in the rear of the APC aft of the turret and two forward of the turret. All were seated in the usual passenger locations. The seventh man was sitting in the commander's old seat just behind the driver, although a simple hatch replaced the commander's cupola.

The turret seats for the commander and the gunner protruded below the hull roof and a pedestal mounted in the centre of the passenger compartment. This pedestal was mostly for the electrical wiring to the turret. Due to the low power output available in the FV432, no power traverse was provided; instead, the turret was hand-cranked. Most of the power was envisioned for the night sight which, if included, would cost some £3,000. The cost of just a Fox turret, without the sight, was given as £7,800. One suggestion to get around this lack of night vision was for the platoon's Carl Gustav recoilless rifle to fire illumination rounds.

There were a few other changes suggested for the turret; first the removal of the commander's cupola as it would add 6in of height and additional weight. The final alteration was to inject a ring sight into the gunner's sight for AA work. This addition is curious because earlier studies had shown that even the best weapon option for AA work would only have a 1 per cent chance of hitting an aircraft. Despite this, the requirement persisted, with one officer stating that 'Crews of approaching aircraft must appreciate offensive action is being taken against them and that this could result in an aircraft kill.'

The Fox turret approach was liked because of the reusable nature of the components. The gun, for example, could be put into other vehicles, such as the MICV-80. In one meeting on 10 March 1967 Major General P.G.F. Young, the newly-appointed DINF, asked if the Fox turrets from the FV432 could be mounted on CVR(T) chassis. Such a contraption did appear, nearly thirty years later, and for different reasons; old FV101 Scorpion hulls were mated with Fox turrets to create the Sabre light tank. As it turned out, only one FV432 per platoon was upgraded to a turret, and just in the Berlin Brigade. However, the MICV-80 was coming along and would soon take over the IFV role with the in-service designation of FV510 Warrior, which would serve the army for many decades.

PART 4

War Rocket

Chapter 13

The Time of the Giants

During the Second World War, the British forces did use at least one direct-fire rocket weapon system: the 'Tulip' kit applied to M4 Sherman tanks of the 1st Coldstream Guards. These were RP-3 aerial rockets taken from a Typhoon squadron with a pair of launching rails welded to the side of the Sherman tank turrets. Aiming was done by the commander, with a vane sight on the roof of the turret. Because the rocket was designed to be flying at several hundred miles per hour when launched from the wing of a Typhoon, the rockets fired on the ground from the Sherman had a significant drop-off while the projectile reached its required speed. To compensate for this, the launch rails had to be fixed in an elevated position, with one on each tank set to 150mm and one to 160mm above the horizontal. This offset meant that one rocket would hit anything in its way up to 400 yards, the other up to 800 yards.

On no occasion was the rocket used against enemy armour; the closest was the use against a towed artillery piece. This lack of armoured opponents was viewed with dissatisfaction among some in the unit, as they were confident that they could remove the turret of any enemy AFV they met. Such confidence was not shared by the DG of A, Major General Otto Lund, who wrote in August 1945 that he saw little prospect of using rockets for any anti-armour work. First, there was the problem of reloading rocket rails outside the tank, and then there was the accuracy. At the time the best high-velocity gun currently available had a mean deviation of 1.2 minutes, which was seen as still being lacking, with the War Office requesting 0.5 minutes. In comparison rockets, such as those on the Sherman Tulips, had an accuracy of 1.2 degrees, which was 62 minutes. The DG of A closed his comments with the following: 'I cannot see the rocket replacing the gun as a precision weapon unless some unforeseen development of it occurs and can only visualise its use as a secondary armament of one-shot weapons for short-ratio fire against fairly massive targets.'

Five years later a new war would break out, one that would cause the technological developments of the rocket that Major General Lund had not been able to foresee previously.

The first weeks of the Korean War were disastrous for the allied forces. Allied armour was either old and worn out, or (as was the case with Australian forces) entirely absent. This led to the large numbers of North Korean tanks overrunning the allied positions with little to stop them. This experience caused the Australians to begin thinking about improving infantry anti-tank weapons. The original idea behind the project was a weapon where each missile could be carried and operated by a single man, and the missile could be remotely guided onto the target after launch. The starting-point for this was the German X-4 guided anti-aircraft missile, developed during the Second World War. The concept behind the project was supported by the development work done by the Germans on the X-7 anti-tank missile. By August 1950 the Australians were making preliminary studies, although they had not placed the weapon on their development programme. At this time, they were also making tentative enquiries to the British to see if they had any similar projects in an attempt to avoid research and development from being duplicated. The British reply indicated that they had been thinking along those lines; however, they had not yet got anything under development. An outline specification was requested from the British as a starting-point for the Australian project. Initially, the Department for Weapons Design was extremely sceptical about the weapon, citing its high cost and the probably extremely high cost of training. There were also doubts based on the German experiences with the X-7, which showed that at closer ranges the weapon was difficult to aim at its target.

However, in Britain, the DG of A was in support of the idea and pressed forward. Equally, he received support from other areas of government that felt that a project of this magnitude would result in an upgrade to Australia's manufacturing and scientific development capabilities. At the time the British were just starting, and the idea of a smaller lighter weapon that could be fitted to tanks was indeed very attractive. Equally, for the infantry – which can deploy into terrain that a tank unit cannot – being able to be armed with that level of firepower would be of interest.

To that end, the outline specification was issued on the chance that something might come of it. The specifications called for a weapon that set armour penetration above all else; the target given for the weapon to defeat was 6in sloped at 60 degrees. Accuracy was required to be able to hit a 7.5ft square target 80 per cent of the time at a range of 1,000 yards. This was seen as the minimum allowed maximum range. Recognizing the issues with guided weapons, the specification also called for the weapon to be entirely under control by 200 yards.

As the weapon had to be man-portable, there were strict limits on weight. The maximum weight for the weapon was 35lb per missile, and all components should be able to be carried by a single man for a few hundred yards. The specifications did recognize that the launcher might need to be broken down into two loads for this.

With this as a starting-point, the Australians initiated a development programme which they named 'Malkara', or 'Shield' in one of the Aboriginal languages. Progress moved with startling speed, and by February 1951 the first prototype had been constructed. The pace of development may have been down to the Australians and British

The Malkara missile and its launching arm. The shape of the arm is somewhat unusual and attaches to the top rear of the missile. No document seen has explained this series of decisions, although the large wings would likely negate an arm from the sides.

establishing a rocket development site at Woomera in 1946, which was headed up by the brilliant Dr W. Alan Butement. Dr Butement was one of the co-discoverers of radar in 1931 and had designed the radar proximity fuse during the Second World War. Dr Butement migrated to Australia in 1949 after taking up the role of Chief Scientist of the Australian Department of Supply and was instrumental in the development of Malkara. By 1 April 1951, a second prototype was under construction. However, the first prototype had been damaged during wind tunnel testing. Prototype control equipment was ready for its testing and supplies of rocket motors were prepared. A total of twelve prototypes were under construction. These would be used for firings and were re-usable, and instead of carrying a live warhead the missiles were fitted with a parachute in the nose. After the missile hit the target, which was a canvas screen, it could then be steered upwards to an altitude of about 100ft, at which point the parachute would deploy and hopefully the missile could be retrieved and re-used.

Test firings were to be conducted at Woomera, and seven of the prototypes were due to arrive on 8 October 1951. There was at least one official visit by a British officer before the end of 1951, although the exact dates are not recorded. The officer's name was Colonel Offord. By that time there had been some eighty launches of missiles. Colonel Offord describes the prototype weapons as weighing in at some 200lb total weight. These components form a missile with a 56lb HESH warhead, of which 40lb was explosive. A production version was produced in February 1952, with eight missiles forecast to be delivered to Woomera in March.

For the first two seconds after launch, covering a distance of about 300 yards, the missile was programmed to fly straight, at a slight angle, to clear the launcher and any obstructions, after which it would settle down to be above the line of sight and be controllable out to its maximum range of 1,500 yards. All the gunner needed to do at that point was to bring the tracer at the back of the missile down into his gun sight, which was termed 'gathering up'. After having a session on the inbuilt simulator and watching fourteen other launches, Colonel Offord was allowed to fire a live missile. His shot fell short of the target by about 80 yards, ricocheted through the target and hit a camera costing around £4,000.

Above and below: The view from the range camera sited behind the target as a Malkara approaches and rips through the dead centre.

Of the previous missiles fired, ten were direct hits on targets equating to 6ft, two were near misses and two failed due to malfunctioning rockets. The defects in these rockets were known faults and were to be remedied shortly. Another flaw that had occurred once in the eighty firings was a malfunctioning tracer element that had burned through the control wire.

The simulator that Colonel Offord mentioned was a 9in cube that was going to be fitted to every launcher. It projected a dot of light into the reticle to simulate the flare at the back of the missile. This dot could be steered in exactly the same way as a missile. The dot would slowly dim to represent the missile getting further away. As this equipment was fitted to every launcher, the crews of that launcher could conduct training exercises whenever they felt like it, with no need to expend a very costly missile.

Repeated firings were discovering new faults even in the production version. One missile that was fired on Thursday, 21 August 1952 was launched at an angle of +50 degrees. During gathering up the operator over-corrected as he brought the missile down, so he immediately brought the missile upwards with a sharp manoeuvre, which caused the wire to bunch up, then tighten within the spools, with the result that all four wires broke at the same time and the missile became uncontrollable.

The missile itself was 62.3in long, with a wingspan of 42.1in. Each pair of wings pivoted together through 15 degrees to steer the missile and could be dismounted for transport. The wings were controlled by low-pressure air taken from the forward fairing and then piped back to power the pivot mechanism.

The missile was constructed of three sections: the warhead, a 6in square body containing the actuator and control systems, and the tail section containing the wire spool and rocket motors. The rockets came in two versions. The first to fire was the boost rocket, designated as 'No.1 tail, propelling rocket, 2in Mk 6', and was mounted in the centre of the tail section. Two wire spools were mounted symmetrically around it, containing some 1,750 yards of wire. The boost rocket produced a force of 500lb/sec and would accelerate the missile to about 300fps in one second, and then burn out after 1.5 seconds. The next stage contained a pair of sustaining rockets, which would fire after the boost rocket had completed its burn.

Each sustaining rocket produced 11lb of thrust, which was sufficient to maintain the missile at 300fps for another fifteen seconds, which was

A Ferret armoured car mounting an unknown British missile, showing the sheer size of these weapons. The weapon is obviously of Malkara stock due to the launching arm being nearly identical. It has been suggested that this is an early prototype of Orange William, but this was just speculation.

enough to reach the 1,500-yard range. It was envisioned that the range could be increased to 2,000 yards with ease should it be required. As it turned out the Mk 1A version of the missile, which was the version that entered service in 1960, had its range increased to nearly 4,000 yards.

During the period there was another anti-tank guided missile being developed: the French SS10. The British started negotiating for a batch of these missiles sometime in 1951, but a year later nothing had come of it and there was a push to close the deal. There were some concerns about creating bad faith in the French if they sealed the deal on the SS10s, then shortly afterwards unveiled the Malkara. Equally the Australians were keen to learn about French experiences. However, the British saw the French as politically insecure and unreliable and were unwilling to give the Australian data to the French. They did suggest to the Australians that should a demonstration of the SS10 be carried out that they could smuggle an Australian observer or two into the event as part of the British delegation. As it was, the British did intend to notify the French of the existence of the project should the deal for SS10s be completed and would share some of the missiles with Australia.

Part of the interest in the French missile was that while Malkara did seem to work, it was a very heavy missile. Towards the end of 1951 the UK began to review its anti-tank policies, and this review included anti-tank guided missiles. Part of this review included the British 'Project E' which was being developed concurrently in the UK; this was a 70lb missile with a 15lb warhead. It seems that as a result of the review the development of both was combined with development primarily conducted at Woomera. In August 1952 a lightweight version of Project E was under development, with such measures as building parts of the missile out of cardboard. Confusingly, both this weapon and Malkara were termed the 'Australian anti-tank weapon' in British documents. The lightweight Project E started with a request for details of an 8lb warhead. It is likely that this was a HEAT warhead instead of HESH. HESH was originally selected for the same reasons that the previously mentioned 183mm gun was selected, because it was the only type of warhead that could ensure disruption, not destruction. With attention turning to HEAT, efforts were made to determine the most suitable dimensions of the warhead. Investigation showed that the effects of a 3.5in cone were insufficient to achieve the destruction of a tank, while a 4in cone was marginally effective. However, a HEAT warhead with a 4.5in-diameter cone would result in the satisfactory destruction of contemporary tanks. Additionally, a 4.5in cone warhead would weigh about 8lb. This was seen as a major improvement as the original specifications had asked for an all-up weight of 35lb per missile, which the current missile considerably exceeded.

The 1951 review included the idea of creating an 'artillery' version of the missile. This was to be a larger weapon, which used wire spooling to set its range and allow the warhead to detonate at a predetermined range. The warhead was envisioned as a downward-facing shrapnel round, which would act as an air burst above any target in cover.

Malkara was to have its own dedicated launching vehicle. An early idea, around August 1951, was to have a Universal Carrier fitted with eight missiles. One wonders how such a contraption would look considering the size of the Malkara. It seems likely that detailed planning

Model of the fighting compartment of the FV4010. The missile bodies are in the racks towards the front of the fighting compartment. Some of the missile bodies are modelled partially extracted. With the arm towards the rear of the compartment the crew could slide a missile body directly back onto the launching arm, then quickly fit the wings from the locations shown before rotating the butterfly hatch to bring the missile into the ready-to-fire position.

of a launcher vehicle was postponed for several years while efforts were concentrated on the development of the missile to obtain a more exact idea of what the launcher vehicle would need.

In 1955 detailed work on the Malkara launching vehicle was begun. The vehicle was based on the Centurion tank. The tank resembles a Centurion that is reversing, with the engine to the front and a casemate placed covering the fighting compartment. The front of the tank had the engine in it and was protected by a glacis that was 200mm thick, and a lower nose plate that was 100mm. The sides were 50mm with 6mm skirting plates. The casemate had its front sloped at 50 degrees and was 180mm thick. At the back of the casemate was a launching arrangement;

The full-scale mock-up with the butterfly hatch in action; it is currently rotating a readied missile into position. On the other side of the hatch is the arm that has just fired a missile and is disappearing down into the fighting compartment to be re-loaded.

this could traverse through 30 degrees either side of the centreline. The launching equipment consisted of a rotating butterfly hatch, with two launching arms on opposite sides of the hatch. This arrangement meant that when one arm was in the raised ready-to-fire position the other would be inside the crew compartment, which allowed the crews to work on assembling the next missile while one was either about to be or had been launched. Using a mock-up, under ideal conditions, crews at Woomera got the reload time down 15.5 seconds. However, the expected in-service rate of fire was two rounds per minute.

By 1960 how to employ Malkara was under consideration. In that year a series of trials were carried out by BAOR using simulated Malkaras, including light armoured cars carrying the weapon and some simulated FV4010s. Also under consideration was to examine the idea of replacing one Centurion per troop with an FV4010. The results were unsurprising, in that the Malkara worked best with open terrain and at long ranges.

The same year also marked the start of the service life of the Malkara, although not on the FV4010. The main attraction with even a heavy missile like the Malkara was that when compared to an anti-tank gun

One of Cyclops Squadron's Hornets with its arm extended and two missiles ready to fire, while on exercise. Again the sheer size of the Malkara becomes apparent from this view.

it was light and mobile. From this, the missile seemed like a piece of ideal equipment for paratroops. To that end, the RAC decided to form its air-portable squadron in 1960. Early in the year, the FV1620 Hornet was selected to be the new squadron's launching vehicle. The RAC was of the opinion that a better vehicle could be designed; however, logistics forced their hand. As the resupply vehicles and the test vehicle were all based upon the FV1611 Humber Pig, it made sense for the launcher vehicle to be on the same chassis.

The Hornet carried four missiles, two ready to fire on the retractable boom at the rear of the vehicle and two reload missiles. However, it was not possible to parachute drop or air-land a Hornet with missiles on the launcher arms. The first four prototypes were constructed during 1960, with one being received by the FVRDE later in the year, just in time for that year's RAC conference, which allowed it to be used in a demonstration. To give the delegates a chance to see what being under missile attack was like, the weapon was to be fired towards them, although not directly at them. The first production vehicle was planned to begin arriving in April 1962, which would coincide with the first troops of the air-portable squadron becoming operational, although this date slipped to November. The squadron was formed in October 1961 and comprised volunteers from 2RTR. Due to the need for a single regiment to find soldiers of sufficient calibre to be parachutists as well, only one troop of the squadron was to be air-portable, although this requirement was later expanded to include the entire squadron. Each Hornet had a crew of three. The vehicle commander was the gunner and trained to the highest level. These were termed 'first controllers', and were usually NCOs. During training, they would fire five missiles. Second controllers and all officers of the squadron would get to fire two of the limited stock of missiles. The third man was the driver and also trained to fire the weapon. First and second controllers would have to fire some 800 simulator shots, using either a dedicated facility or the built-in simulator. The biggest problem experienced by the Malkara squadron was in getting candidates through both parachute training and guided weapon training. The best candidates for first controllers and the role of vehicle commander were the experienced NCOs. These would, of course, be older men and thus they would struggle with the parachute training. The squadron commander, Ian Baker, admitted in his worst moments that he thought he would get two groups of men, one qualified as parachutists and the other trained as first controllers. By placing all recruits through parachute training first, they were able to get enough personnel to make the entire squadron parachutable.

The air-portable squadron gained the title of Cyclops Squadron in 1962. Its role was to provide a long-range anti-tank defence to the UK's strategic reserve. It was the first RAC unit to be parachute-capable for fourteen years. The Malkara was seen as an interim ATGM until Swingfire arrived in service; this was projected to happen in the late 1960s. Due to this, Cyclops Squadron was to be the only unit equipped with the Malkara, and due to its short service life and high cost, around £4,000, only a limited number of missiles had been purchased. The squadron consisted of a headquarters unit mounted in Land Rovers; three guided weapons (GW) troops equipped with Hornets. There was an administrative troop, mounted on Humber Pigs. This troop was the ammo resupply formation carrying reloads. Each GW troop would normally have one or two ammunition vehicles attached from the administrative troop. Next was the test troop: this consisted of two vehicles with trailers and was not parachutable. The test equipment was designed so that each missile was plugged into diagnostic equipment and would give a go/no-go result. It would not state what was wrong with the missile. If the missile passed this test, it was handed over to the administrative troop for transport to a launcher. If it failed, it was moved to the final troop of the squadron, which was the LAD section mounted in Land Rovers.

There were some teething troubles with Malkara and the Hornet. On the Malkara the fuse was causing some problems and would set the missile's introduction date back to May 1963. In the case of the Hornet, the lack of remote unit that allowed the first controller to launch and control the missile from about 80 yards away was delayed; this meant that the Hornet was vulnerable to enemy action. The fix for this was due to arrive in July 1964.

In the 1960s the army was faced with the ageing Malkara, and therefore the Hornet, wasting out of service before AVR was ready. If this happened, the army would have no long-range ATGM in service until the much-delayed replacement finally arrived. To combat this capability gap, the army looked at the cost of buying a second batch of Malkaras. This purchase came out at the cost of £4,500 per missile; in comparison adapting Hornet to carry Swingfire would cost £6,000 to £7,500 per vehicle. This modified Hornet would mount six launchers

A Hornet undergoing a test firing. Attached to the rear wheel hub there is some form of sensor, and wires leading off to the right of the camera.

on its arm, and carry four reloads. It is likely that the delays in the Swingfire project that pushed the missile's in-service date further back towards a point where both the launching vehicle and the missile would enter service at the same time meant that the Hornet conversion was dropped.

The Orange William missile started life in 1956 when Fairey Aviation Co. was given the go-ahead to develop the missile. Weighing in at a massive 223lb, it bore a strong resemblance to the Malkara with the same basic layout. Although it was much longer, being 86.5in in length, the wingspan was only 34in. The pneumatic power for the wing controls was provided from a 3,000lb/psi compressed air bottle. The 60lb warhead contained 37lb of plastic explosive. The significant change for the missile was the split from wire control to an infrared beam serving as the link. The solid fuel rocket had two stages, with a boost phase lasting one second ramming this mass of a missile up to 500fps, then the sustainer rocket would take over, which lasted thirty-nine seconds. This time was enough to carry the missile some 6,000 yards. However, the maximum engagement range was to be limited to 4,000 yards. This range was to allow the missile controller to be up to 2,000 yards closer than the launcher vehicle. The split between the launcher and the controller was called 'separation'. Because the launcher and controller had to be within a line of each other there needed to be some knowledge of where each other was located; it was found that simple map-reading skills with 1/25,000 scale maps were sufficient. There was provision being made for an emergency signal, with the launcher emitting a puff of white smoke to allow the controller team to position itself.

Due to the large amount of separation Orange William provided, it was felt that the launcher could be lightly armoured. A first attempt based upon the FV420 5-ton load carrier failed as the vehicle was not mechanically reliable enough; however, a second vehicle was designed based upon the FV421. This new vehicle was termed Carrier, Tracked, Launcher, FV426, Orange William, projected to be about 17ft 4in long, 8ft 4in tall and 9ft 6in wide and weigh about 15 tons. It was desired that it be proof against a .50 heavy machine gun and artillery bursts within 20ft; to achieve this it was protected by 12mm of IT100 armour on all surfaces. It was also to be able to operate on a battlefield contaminated by nuclear weapons.

There was a crew of four: a commander, driver and two loaders, the latter because the launcher vehicle had two launching arms. These were sighted in the side of the tank on a beam arrangement behind two side doors, which allowed the launchers to be retracted inside the vehicle and the launching door sealed so that the loader could assemble a missile on the launcher. Then when ready he would open his door and slide the beam and launcher outside. The beam could then be rotated, in the vertical, to the desired angle for launch. Two ramps from the ammunition storage would lead to the launchers. The ammunition storage was over the rear engine containing two racks, holding five missile bodies between them. The bodies would be complete missiles with warheads. Fins and tails would be stored in the front, on either side of the vehicle. Thus, the loader could slide a missile down the ramp onto the launcher, and then attach the missile. He would then affix the wings and tails. The total number of missiles carried was seven. Should the missile be faulty, the arm could be extended and the missile jettisoned. The rate of fire for this complex operation was given as three rounds in the first minute and then two missiles thereafter. Other weapons carried would be a pair of Bren guns which could be fired from ports dotted around the vehicle to give 360-degree cover. In the case of an emergency, the FV426 was fitted with its own missile controller so it could aim and fire its own weapons.

The Orange William missile control system needed two people to operate it. The first aimed at the target and steered the missile, while the second tracked the missile to allow the infrared beam to lock onto the missile and relay control instructions. At first, the controller was to be developed in three stages. The first stage was the control equipment being fitted to a Centurion tank. Next was to provide the tank with a remote unit that could be operated up to 200 yards away and connected by wire. The final stage was to provide a man-pack controller, although this was never realized due to the weight of the equipment; indeed it was suggested that the crew of the man-pack version might need a trolley just to move the batteries. Later it was realized that having a fully-armed and equipped tank acting as a controller for the missile was a waste. A plan was drawn up to fit the controller to a three-man version of the Ferret armoured car, which would give the mobility to get into a

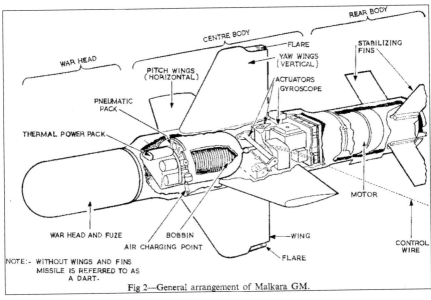

Fig 2—General arrangement of Malkara GM.

Above and Below: Cutaway plans for both Malkara and Orange William. One can immediately see the similarities, and how Orange William looks very like a scaled-up Malkara.

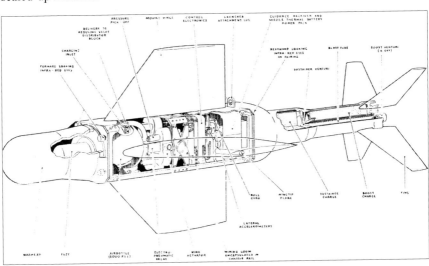

position and the size to be easily concealed and, should it be necessary, the speed to withdraw.

In September 1959, the Orange William project was cancelled. The reasons given for this were that the project was too technically

Artist's impression of the FV426 Orange William. The artist based this vehicle on the FV420 load carrier with added armour and the unique reloading and launching arrangement as described by a document.

advanced, which in turn would raise costs. Malkara was bought as the interim guided weapon, again due mainly to the missile's cheapness. This limited buy of systems would serve until about 1968 when the system would waste out of service, and in turn be replaced by a new missile called Swingfire.

Chapter 14

Swings and Roundabouts

Although Orange William had been cancelled due to the technology behind it being too advanced, the concepts behind it were still seen as desirable. Some £250,000 per year was budgeted for the RARDE to continue development and research into these ideas. The RARDE started Project 12 to keep the development going. This project covered two missiles: a mysterious missile called Quickfire and the Swingfire. Of the former almost no details can be found; in short order, the technology behind it was deemed untenable and the development halted. As Orange William had been cancelled this had deprived Fairey Aviation of a source of income. Fearing a hardship claim from that company, along with their experience with guided weapons the MOD issued a development contract to Faireys for Swingfire in October 1959.

In July 1961 the United States and the UK conducted talks and came to an agreement on anti-tank guided weapons. This understanding was known as the Rubel-Zuckerman agreement, named after Sir Solly Zuckerman, the chief scientist to the MOD, and John H. Rubel. This agreement outlined the areas of research and was an attempt to prevent the United States from developing a competitor to the UK's Swingfire. Some of the points agreed were the following:

- The United States could develop anti-tank weapons for close to medium-range weapons, which were defined as weapons with a range up to 1,000m, but these could be given guidance systems
- No competitor to the Swingfire and Vigilant systems would be developed
- The United States could experiment with anti-tank guided weapons but would consult with the UK before undertaking development
- The United States would investigate a range of advanced anti-tank assault weapon concepts; however, United States programmes would not compete with Swingfire and Vigilant.

Shortly afterwards in August 1961 Swingfire received its GSOR, numbered 1013, which called for a wire-guided system with a range of 4,000m. As a guided missile has a small range before its warhead has armed and the missile has come under guidance it was decided that if the missile has a slow launch, then this distance will be very low. In the case of Swingfire, the minimum range was just 140m. The GSOR also called for allowing separation between launcher and controller. The missile had an initial launch of only 3G and used a vectored thrust which allowed it remarkable manoeuvrability, able to turn 45 degrees after launch; this was a pre-programmed flight path designed to bring it within the sight picture of the controller within 70m. Then he would control it for the rest of its fourteen-second flight for medium range, or twenty-four seconds for long range. This ability to manoeuvre is what caused the system to be called Swingfire. Another unique feature of Swingfire was that it automatically gathered the missile.

The original Swingfire was to have a 4,000m range; however, it was also desired to have a medium-range version with just 2,000m range. This reduced range would, it was hoped, save weight and allow the missile to be man-packed. The medium-range Swingfire was also sometimes called the infantry or INSWING version, while the long-range one was called the RAC Swingfire. It was agreed by the United States and Canada to add this medium-range missile to the priority standardization list for all three countries.

The Rubel-Zuckerman agreement lasted a few months before the United States attempted to end it. The US bids to cancel the deal became such a contentious problem that it was elevated for discussion between Harold Macmillan and John F. Kennedy. By 1962 the United States had started work on the TOW system. In May the United States suggested that the British leave the field of guided weapons research to them as the TOW was suitably advanced, and the French were also developing a competitor. The United States pointed out that three United States companies, namely Hughes, McDonnell and Martin, had undertaken 'feasibility' studies on the weapon system. However, each firm had invested at least three times the funding allocated by the United States government to the project and was ready to fly at least five missiles each between 10 and 20 July.

Hughes' entry was a missile controlled by pop-out fins powered pneumatically to control pitch and yaw, while a gyroscope controlled the roll of the missile. The rocket motor was built by Hercules, while the wire dispenser came from Bofors. Hughes themselves would be producing the

IR flare and sensor. During this period the Hughes' main problems were the aerodynamics of the unfolding wings and getting the IR to work.

The McDonnell entry fired a missile that was to spin like a standard shell. Guidance was achieved by sighting the IR sensor in a long V-shaped trough on the control unit. As the gravity pulls the missile downwards, its IR flare moves towards one side of the V, at which point the thruster on that side is fired to push it away. The direction was determined by a gyroscope to sense the orientation of the missile, which gave the projectile a wobbly flight path, with the missile bouncing upwards by 2ft every 400m.

Martin's missile did not spin; instead, it had a pair of swept-back fins, and at the centre of gravity two nozzles slanted downwards to sustain the missile. A further arrangement of nozzles would control the flight path.

All the designs could accept an unguided rocket that was to be used if a target was at close range. The TOW was sometimes referred to as a Heavy Assault Weapon, in counterpoint to the M72 LAW; it is likely the term assault weapon was specifically chosen as the development of those was allowed under the Rubel-Zuckerman agreement.

All these features meant that the gunner had to remain with the TOW launcher and aim the missile; this lack of separation was a major sticking-point between the United States' and UK developments, as the UK absolutely required it while the United States felt it was utterly irrelevant. The United States also claimed that the TOW project was a fallback in case the Shillelagh missile failed in its development; indeed, the first TOW missiles even mounted the same warhead.

The main reason for this disagreement was the difference in equipment policies. Before the Swingfire the UK had a series of weapons such as the Energa grenade for section anti-tank and a 3.5in recoilless launcher at platoon level to cover out to 1,000m. To cover from 1,000m out to 2,000m there were WOMBAT and Vigilant missiles, although the missile was the longest range of the two with only 1,350m reach. Over 2,000m tank guns would provide anti-tank firepower. The United States was following a similar doctrine with the M72 LAW 90mm recoilless rifle and the ENTAC missile, which the TOW would replace. After 1965 the UK planned to have a single weapon, the Carl Gustav recoilless rifle, to cover out to 150m, after which the Swingfire would take over out to 2,000m.

The RAC needed the longer-range Swingfire for engaging tanks at long range, and so had produced GSOR 1007 which called for the Swingfire to be mounted on a Chieftain. Thirty-six tanks in each regiment would be equipped with the missile system. This mount was to enable the Chieftain to be able to kill heavy tanks at over 2,000m and thin out tank attacks. It was also expected that self-propelled guns would give any Soviet attack overwatch cover from their start line; the Swingfire was seen as an answer to these as well. By October 1962 it was decided to cancel the requirement to fit the weapon to Chieftain. The reasons for this cancellation were based on several factors such as the cost: the weapon would cost £60,000 to develop and each installation would cost £10,000. The equipment was bulky and vulnerable to enemy action and only carried four missiles, with no reloads. It was also seen as overworking the commander and adding complications to the commander's sight. Finally, and most importantly, the 120mm L11 gun was proving to be far more powerful and capable than had initially been foreseen.

Despite the range and hitting power of the Chieftain's main gun, the need for the Swingfire in RAC units was still foreseen, thus in November 1962 GSOR 1174 was issued, which called for a long-range anti-tank guided weapon launcher vehicle. Almost immediately the FV432 was given the role, with the resulting vehicle being the FV438 Swingfire. A year later the FV438 was still under development; the primary choice in the design that had to be taken was what to do with the rocket efflux when the missile was fired. At the end of October 1963, it was decided to use forward efflux, where the exhaust left the launcher with the missile, allowing the FV438 to appear outwardly identical to a normal FV432. In the forward efflux design, the twin launcher racks were attached to the roof by a single pivot point. When elevated to 45 degrees the missile box's lower lip would be level with the roof. The launcher could then be lowered and would face downwards by a few degrees to allow the loader, who knelt on the floor in front of the launchers, to load from the fourteen spare missiles stored under the launcher.

The Ministry of Aviation then started conducting testing on the forward efflux system. The results caused such alarm that on 27 February the Ministry issued a paper that recommended the abandonment of forward efflux. The reasons for this were twofold. When fired, the missile generated an 8ft plume of flame that lasted for half a second. This badly scorched the command wire and could damage the rear of the missile. More alarmingly, on a simulated hang-fire, the missile set a fire that was so violent that after three minutes with no sign of the flames abating the trials' department had to extinguish the fire. In the same tests after a relatively short amount of time, the fire was judged to have penetrated

An FV438 launches yet another missile. It is apparent that this FV438 has fired several times as there are wires just visible draped over the front of the tank. This shot shows off the action of the wire-catcher just forward of the launcher.

the fighting compartment through the launching box. With the racks for reloads stored directly under the launcher box, it would almost certainly result in the destruction of the vehicle.

With the forward efflux being cancelled there was a brief study on rear efflux mountings. At first, the idea was to keep the same set-up as with the forward efflux version, only vent directly out of the rear of the vehicle. This, however, meant a significant modification of the FV432, whereas the forward efflux version was just a bolt-on change to the mortar hatch and could be fitted with ease. As this would increase the cost, it was decided not to adopt this solution. Instead, the mortar hatch was replaced with a small superstructure and two launchers that laid flat on the roof and could be accessed from the superstructure. The launchers were hinged at their base and could elevate to the required 45 degrees. This arrangement also gave the added advantage of allowing the loader to stand, improving the ergonomics of lifting the heavy missiles. This was the arrangement that would eventually enter service.

It will have been noted in the previous section that the Ministry of Aviation was conducting the testing of the forward efflux system. This was because of the set of circumstances that added to the development misery that plagued the Swingfire project. In 1957 a defence review was conducted

The in-service version of the FV438 shows off the rear efflux arrangement designed to overcome a lot of the problems that were encountered during the design phase of the vehicle.

by the government. A significant part of this review was to amalgamate several companies into larger entities. Faireys were not to be part of these mergers, and so the MOD wanted the development to be carried out by the British Aircraft Corporation as part of a rationalization of missiles and aviation. Faireys were understandably unhappy with this, and it took several months to negotiate the transfer. BAC suffered a setback when the Blue Water tactical nuclear missile was cancelled in August 1962, which caused their Luton factory to close and meant 1,500 redundancies at Stevenage. To eliminate many of these losses, Swingfire development was moved to Stevenage from Heston. However, it was done in such haste that many of the Swingfire team refused to relocate as they lacked confidence in the project. Stevenage also required a refit with many of its machining tools having to be modified for the new missile. The launching equipment development was sent to BAC's Filton factory, which cost another six months. In an attempt to fix the problems, the Vigilant project leader was switched to Swingfire, and the company's chief engineer was to look at the designs to see if he could spot any flaws in an independent review.

The development had many problems, the most serious being with the hot gas servo valve that suffered a build-up of dirt which caused it to fail.

The reason was tracked to gas generator charge, which had an inhibitor compound in it to promote even burning. This inhibitor was part of the problem. After altering the design of the servo valve slightly, twelve test firings were conducted followed by three tethered launches, all of which were successful. The problem was that to achieve these an inhibitor had to be used that could not meet the GSOR's storage requirements and would cause the missile to have a very short shelf life. Knowing that this would be unacceptable to the army, BAC was desperately searching for a replacement inhibitor. One of the reasons cited for this problem was that while developing the engine, all the development had been done with compressed air. To add to the technical problems the gyroscope also caused excessive vibration that caused the missile to be unstable, and the electronics pack needed to be rearranged.

Fiscally the project was in trouble as well. Originally Faireys had forecast that development would cost £3 million; they added a 50 per cent contingency to that and then rounded off to £5 million. They revised this to £5.5 million in April 1962. The Treasury only approved £3.91 million and stated should the contingency be needed, it should be applied for. By 1965 the costs were up to £7.2 million. Expenditure continued to rise through 1966 to £8.3 million, until finally, by 1969, the expenses hit £9.5 million. From 1965 the Treasury had been insisting on regular project reviews and causing the project to be resubmitted for approval several times.

There were other troubles with the programme that added to the time taken to get the missile into service, with evaluation trials originally scheduled for July 1962 and an in-service date of early 1966. By August 1964 the start of the trials was set as January 1966. By October 1964 Swingfire had not actually had a successful launch. Equally, on 7 November 1964, the medium-range Swingfire was cancelled due to the inability to lower the weight of the missile sufficiently. All these problems caused the MOD to become very concerned, especially at the reactions of BAC, and it resulted in a series of meetings between Lord Caldecote, the owner of BAC, and a number of senior army figures who pressed the seriousness of the situation upon him.

It might have been of some comfort to the MOD officials involved in the Swingfire programme that the United States TOW project, now with the designation HM-88, was encountering difficulties. In a presentation in 1964 the United States laid out details of its TOW programme and some of the challenges they were facing. Most were of the minor technical nature that appear in any project; however, there was a considerable amount of smoke being generated when the TOW was fired. At this time the United States was hoping to get 3,000m range but realized that the accuracy beyond 2,000m would be awful. Another feature that had been dropped was the unguided projectile part of the design. The parent company, Hughes, were also undertaking an assessment of the ability of TOW against aircraft, despite the United States army not wanting or needing the TOW in such a role. The previous year the RARDE had looked at using Swingfire in the AA role, and very quickly realized that it would be useless; not just from the difficulties of obtaining a hit but from the lack of lethality from the HEAT warhead against aircraft. The MOD was forced to make the point about the lack of lethality against non-armoured targets in June 1964 when a delegation was dispatched to give a presentation on Swingfire to Sweden. The Swedes were looking at a guided missile for anti-shipping work as part of their coastal defences. They were extremely interested in the ability of the missile to automatically gather up, making training of operators much easier. Because of the Swedes' intended target, it was suggested that Malkara would be more suitable.

Finally, on 30 April 1969, the evaluation trials for Swingfire were completed. The hit accuracy was only 80 per cent at short range and 60 per cent at long range. This performance fell short of the GSOR's call for 90 per cent and 85 per cent respectively. In addition, the training aids were considered substandard as well as a host of minor faults. Even so, in June it was advised that the missile be accepted into service. After consideration, the army refused to accept the missile for release to service on 28 July. The army stated that when the accuracy was within 5 to 10 per cent of the GSOR and the training equipment deficiencies were fixed, it would release to service.

Finally, after repeated assurances from the parent company that fixes would be developed, along with a steadily increasing number of successful launches, the Swingfire was released to service in August. The main cause of lack of accuracy was the smoke ejected by the motor, which was significant. Reduced smoke motors were to be introduced in 1972. The problem with the missile's gyro drifting off was solved by increasing the angle of the launchers by 3 degrees. The igniter was also causing problems, but a solution was in hand. One final problem was that the Swingfire could not be fired over salt water. It has been suggested that as salt water is more conductive than fresh water, the exposure would cause faults, even triggering the command break-up in which the missile would self-destruct

The FV102 Striker launching a Swingfire missile. Based on the CVRT chassis, this highly-mobile vehicle would mount the Swingfire for many years and continue to serve even when the FV438 was withdrawn from service. It was this vehicle that would carry the Swingfire until 2005 when it, along with the Swingfire, was finally withdrawn from service.

as a safety measure if it lost contact with its base unit. Another theory that has been put forward is that the exhaust, when mixed with salt water, would create hydrochloric acid, which would erode and dissolve the wires. Either way, no documents back up or even state what the problem was with the salt water environment, so this should be treated as a hypothesis.

The salt water problem continued until at least March 1972, when an epoxy coat for the wires was being trialled. It appears that this experiment would eventually be successful. This coating along with a technical development gave rise to two new projects relating to Swingfire. GSOR 1013 had also included the option for mounting the Swingfire on a helicopter. However, if a specific control fault occurred during launch, then the missile would strike the launching vehicle, with catastrophic and deadly results. This led, along with some doctrinal questions, to the idea not being pursued during the lengthy and expensive development. In 1972 the MOD issued a research contract to BAC to solve the safety problem. In addition, a vehicle altitude reference unit was being incorporated along with a stabilized gunner's sight.

171

The missile cases were also being re-engineered to become a tube with a frangible nose cone. As well as mounting on a helicopter, the MOD issued a research contract to the British Hovercraft Corporation (BHC) to install Swingfire on an SR.N6 hovercraft.

It was found to be entirely feasible to mount four ready missiles and several reloads inside the vehicle, along with a conning tower for a controller. Separation could also be included with relative ease. The idea was for the hovercraft to be either beached, floating or hovering while firing its missiles. As well as the conning tower, the hovercraft also needed a couple of blast deflectors added behind the missile launchers to protect the superstructure. Of note was the idea to skew both launchers 30 degrees away from the centreline, which gave the ability to cover 180 degrees of arc with at least two missiles while maintaining the ability to fire four forwards.

Although the SR.N6 would ultimately be bought and in service with the Royal Navy, the Swingfire mount would never be adopted. Some overseas users have accepted into service something similar, as there are recent reports of Iranian SR.N6 hovercraft being fitted with some form of missile armament.

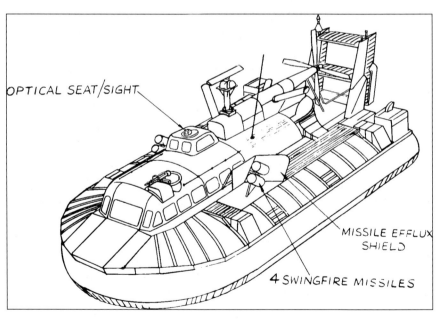

Plans for the SR.N6, with Swingfire mounts. A raised conning tower has been added midway along the roof to mount the sights. The hull would contain several reloads if need be, although replacing the missiles in combat may have been tricky.

Chapter 15

Foiled Again

This part of the book started with concerns about the relative inaccuracy of rockets and how they led to the development of the guided missile. In the late 1950s the problem of rocket inaccuracy once again came under scrutiny, this time for free-flight artillery rockets. Sometime during 1958, a study was undertaken on rockets, and it identified three main contributing factors to rocket inaccuracy. These were errors during launching, surface crosswind effects and thrust misalignment. The British thought they could overcome these challenges and get a really accurate rocket. To remove these negative factors a high-speed motor was selected; this would get the rocket out of the crosswinds before they could have a significant effect on the trajectory. In addition, the motor was of a brand-new design which prevented asymmetrical gas flow to the nozzle, which caused the thrust misalignment. As the five-year study was nearing its end, in June of 1962 GST 17: General Support Medium Artillery was issued. This target called for a weapon able to bombard targets of importance, specifically harder targets than would typically be expected of artillery, as well as being used for counter-battery fire. The GST allowed for either rocket or conventional tube artillery to fulfil the role.

With the previous unnamed study winding up, a new study was created by the RARDE and it was approved in November 1963. Named Project Jawl, it was to run for three years with the aim of meeting the GST 17 requirements. Project Jawl had the experimental rocket from the previous study as its base projectile, which was named FFR-1 and was of 6in diameter. A 7in rocket named FFR-2 was also used in the study; the latter rocket was seen as the service weapon. It had a 25 to 30km range, and initially the burn time of the rocket motor was 0.3 seconds, generating a thrust of 5,500-6,000psi. There were concerns about pressures this high, so the burn time was lengthened to 0.4 seconds which lowered the pressure to 3,700-4,500psi. This, however, meant that the rocket was too long, so the total length was reduced by 16in to 114in, and the burn time lengthened again to 0.43 to compensate. This alteration was sufficient to propel the 300lb (later 350lb) FFR-2, carrying a 100lb warhead, to Mach 3. The wingspan was 19.2in.

Even with the new designs of motor, the rockets were still showing considerable inaccuracy. The cause was traced to the fins of the rocket. At supersonic speeds, the rapidly-expanding motor efflux was creating a detached shockwave, which meant that the airflow over the fins was drastically reduced. The simple expedient of moving the fins forward by 10in solved this. Crosswinds were still having an impact on the rocket's accuracy. To combat this, notches were cut out of the base of the fins to show less area to any wind and reduce the amount of deviation. This simple change decreased the deviation amount by 50 per cent per 1ft of crosswind. To combat the errors during the launch, at first a curved rail was tried; as the rocket accelerates it is forced onto the rail by centrifugal forces, but in some of the test firing the rear of the rocket lifted during launch. An attempt was made to use mechanical simultaneous release clamps, but with the technology of the time, these were unable to release at precisely the same moment. In the end, a progressive downward-loading system was selected to provide the least amount of error during launch.

During the lifetime of the project, various launchers were constructed. These included a single launch rail on a modified 25-pounder carriage, a twin rail launcher on a Land Rover and an eight-rail launcher. To test ripple firing of rockets, a quad rail launcher was built on a 3.7in heavy AA gun mount, and it was found that with 1.5 seconds between rockets in the salvo there was no disruption to the accuracy. All these changes resulted in a dispersion of just 2-4.5 mils, and the target for the study had been 4.5 mils.

With the rocket and style of launcher rail selected, work turned to the warhead. The target was described as a Soviet Motor Rifle company deployed in a 250m-diameter circle. This company was mounted in the BTR-50P. With this target in mind, the people involved in Project Jawl decided to calculate the best lethality per pound of warhead against such a target. To prevent the study from simply coming to the conclusion that a single massive rocket was the answer, the designers set the upper limit at 350lb. One initial problem encountered was the way in which high-explosive warheads detonate. They spray most of the shrapnel out in a very narrow beam to either side of the warhead. This would mean that if the warhead was on a ballistic path a large portion of the warhead's lethal effect would be wasted, but if the warhead was descending vertically, then the spray of fragments would spread evenly over the area. It was planned to have a 10-degree side beam at an angle of 45 degrees. The increase in lethality from vertical descent was calculated as high as a factor of twelve. To achieve vertical descent, a system of having four drag brakes swing out from the body of the rocket was developed. However, this was found to cause inaccuracy. So the simple method of separating the warhead at the correct distance and allowing it to descend on a parachute was selected. Distance control was also a technical problem to be solved. In an artillery piece, range could be modified by changing the propellant charge, an option that was not available to a rocket. An initial study by Hunting Engineering Ltd suggested that a retardation rocket motor would be too costly and cumbersome. However, by modifying the airflow over the rocket to increase or lower drag, suitable range control could be achieved. To this end, a series of different-shaped rings were produced that could be fitted over the nose and tail to alter the rocket's aerodynamics. After tests, it was found that only three sizes were needed.

The type of warhead was also considered. Normal shrapnel would not affect APCs, which were designed to provide protection against such attack. Pre-Formed Fragment (PFF) warheads were then studied. Flechettes were seen as ideal, but the technical problems of firing them in a consistent manner had not yet been solved. That left a warhead filled with spheres or cubes. Cubes meant more could be carried, but they lacked the armour penetration abilities of spheres. So the warhead that was designed for the FFR-2 held 1,600 0.5in spheres made of Mallory 100, a tungsten alloy. It was calculated in a later study on Foil that a 9in rocket warhead containing 1,750 such fragments would kill 12 per cent of vehicles in the target area, although in that study the target was given as an artillery battery consisting of APCs and SPGs in a 300m x 100m area. A battery salvo of Foil was calculated as destroying 48 per cent of the Soviet artillery battery's vehicles in the same area. Immediately the idea of linking Foil to artillery-spotting radar and using them for counter-battery fire was proposed.

Another type of PFF warhead was designed and tested for the FFR-2, which contained some 20,000 0.25in 1 gram steel balls. This warhead was purely for shrapnel effect against personnel and soft targets. Against the previously described artillery target, such a PFF warhead, it was estimated, would eliminate 78 per cent of the unit's personnel.

For the attack of harder targets, a cluster bomblet warhead was considered. This version contained 220 1.25in HEAT bomblets. One advantage was that it would not need a vertical descent, as a small charge would cut the casing allowing centrifugal forces to throw the bomblets out in a set pattern. While these warheads would be able to kill both tanks and APCs, they would lack the hit rate available to a PFF warhead. Equally, they would have a shortcoming in the ability to create a significant amount of fragmentation, although the idea of creating the case of the HEAT warhead out of notched wire was being investigated.

Originally Project Jawl was to have been a three-year study; however, it was requested to have a one-year extension which was granted, allowing the programme to follow several new avenues. By January 1967 some 225 FFR-1s and ten FFR-2s had been fired in various trials and developments. Another ninety FFR-1s were planned, along with fifty FFR-2s scheduled before the end of the study. These test firings showed up a number of flaws. During the testing of a particular type of fuse, the rocket was fired in adverse weather conditions. Corona discharge built up around the nose cone and caused the fuse to trigger. A few changes to the fuse were made, and another test firing in similar conditions went off without a problem. As well as this, a minimum flight time of 1.6 seconds before the fuse was armed was added as an additional safety feature.

The fuel for these rockets was a plastic propellant conforming to composition RD2428, which contained 14 per cent aluminium. However, RD2428 gave a significant flash upon firing, so in 1966 a non-aluminized compound, RD2432, was tried. This propellant solved the flash problem, but was inferior in performance. The fuels were obtained from two locations for the start of the study. ROF Bridgwater supplied the propellant. Although satisfactory when the rockets were stored, after three months several rockets had suffered a bonding failure in their propellants. From September 1967 the Experimental Rocket Development Establishment (ERDE) supplied the propellants, and these remained stable due to the more tightly-controlled way in which ERDE manufactured their propellants. One critical difference was traced to the level of atmospheric moisture in the factory.

During temperature trials two motors fired at a temperature of –20 degrees failed, exploding near the launchers. It was traced to the propellant failing at lower temperatures. This would become a critical point during discussions on standardization between NATO members.

Before those discussions could start, Project Jawl reached the end of its life and so was terminated in 1968. In May of 1967, a revised version of GST 17 was issued, numbered GST 3019. Finally, in June of 1968 GSR 3427 was issued that called for a General Support Rocket System. To meet this requirement the development work was placed under the name Project Foil. Foil was to be the name of the in-service weapon system.

The RARDE carried out a study on how to deploy the weapon system. They assessed all likely vehicles in service with the British army at the time, both armoured and unarmoured, and considered how to mount the Foil launchers. The designs they drew up were for launchers on the FV433 Abbot, FV4201 Chieftain, FV101 CVRT and M107 in both crewed and uncrewed versions. Wheeled launchers included the Bedford MK 4-ton, AEC Militant Mk 3 10-ton, R101 Portée and a towed carriage. The MICV was also assessed, including a lengthened version with six wheels. This last version was seen as the best option, and it had the added advantage of being an identical chassis to the six-wheeled MICV used as a resupply vehicle.

The MICV mounted eight launching beams. Each beam was 144in long, weighed some 350lb and was surrounded by a lightly-armoured box, 30mm thick and made of aluminium. These provided small-arms protection at 200m and would stop 98 per cent of shrapnel from a 105mm airburst at 30m. These eight beams were carried in a rotating turret on the rear deck. These had an arc of 360-degree traverse and could elevate between 0 and 55 degrees. Due to blast from the rockets, it was recommended only to fire with a 90-degree arc centred on the broadside of each vehicle. An additional restriction was that the commander's cupola limited that to a minimum of 5 degrees over a small part of the full rotation.

The commander was seated in the right hull, behind the engine, while the layer was sitting inside the turret and rotated with it. The driver was at first placed to the commander's left; however, in a later part of the design process for the MICV, the driver was moved forward to be to the left of the engine. The engine itself was calculated as giving 30hp per ton and could drive the vehicle at 50mph.

The next two suitable launchers were considered to be the FV433 Abbot and the MICV in its five-wheeled version, although these had some negative points. For example, it was challenging to provide the Abbot with

Artist's impression of the six-wheeled version of the MICV mounting a Foil launching rack.

a wading ability, and it had a bad payload layout. Against the five-wheeled MICV was the limitation that it only carried six launching beams.

The assessment included the loading gauge for train transport, and this restriction eliminated the Chieftain version as although it could mount more rocket beams on the chassis, they could not fit through a standard tunnel. The FV101 was only able to carry one launching beam, and possibly a reload rocket.

Of the wheeled versions, the launchers could only elevate to 12 degrees for the Bedford and 15 degrees for the AEC. Even with stabilizing jacks, the rotating mass was just too large for the trucks to handle. It was found impossible to fit an armoured cab to the Bedford, although there was an AEC version with an armoured body. This was the Heavy Armoured Command Vehicle that was currently being developed. The armoured cab would weigh 1.6 tons, which in turn would reduce the AEC's twelve-rocket payload by three.

The towed carriage had a single launching beam on it and was designed to be pulled by the Land Rover 101 1-ton 4x4. The chassis and wheels for the towed launcher were based upon the trailer being developed for the same truck. This trailer had a connection to the main drive shaft which meant that the wheels on the limber were also powered. As well as carrying

178

The armoured AEC Foil launcher. The cab was taken from plans for the armoured command vehicle and fitted to the plans of the AEC launcher to give a full impression of what the final vehicle might look like.

a single 7in rocket ready to fire, two reloads were stored on the launcher between the launching beam mount and the wheels and suspension.

To provide logistic support to these rocket batteries, there was a variety of specialist rocket-carrying racks designed that could be fitted to all of the army's planned and current soft-skin vehicles. Of particular note was a framework that could be loaded and unloaded at will from most of the army's generic cargo carriers. This supply frame contained sixteen missiles and a jib for use when extracting and then loading the rockets onto the launcher. The system developed allowed for either a single or pair of rockets to be loaded at any one time.

A similar jib arrangement was mounted on all the supply vehicles designed including the MICV six-wheeled missile carrier, which carried sixteen missiles in its cargo bay. These were secured in four racks of four rockets. Two of the brackets were placed with the nose towards the front and two with the nose to the rear. The roof hatches would fold downwards providing a working platform, and the concept was that two launchers would park either side of the supply vehicle, with all facing in the same direction. Then the launch vehicles would traverse their launchers to 90 degrees facing the supply vehicle, at which point the rockets could be loaded, one at a time.

In all of the above designs, the 7in FFR-2 had been used as a basis; however, by July 1969 when these designs were being drawn up the rockets in the Foil programme had expanded in calibre. Now it was to include 8in, two versions of a 9in, and 10in rockets. The main difference in including the larger rockets would mean a reduction in launch beams. In the case of the towed launcher, it meant the removal of the reloads and the direction of the rocket while under tow being switched from pointing away from the towing vehicle to directly towards it.

Type	Calibre/ Warhead	Length (ft)	Weight (lb)	Wingspan (in)	Missiles carried by MICV-6
25/0	7in PFF	8.814	318.8	18.9	8
	7in Cluster	11.703	304.0		
30/M	8in PFF	11.91	521.6	21.6	6
	8in Cluster	12.853	504.0		
30/Y	9in PFF	11.897	677.6	24.3	5
	9in Cluster	14.914	654.4		
40/Q	9in PFF	13.592	754.2	24.3	5
	9in Cluster	16.995	743.0		
40/G	10in PFF	15.277	997.2	27.0	3
	10in Cluster	17.374	977.6		

The British were considering a relatively small buy of Foil, just enough to equip four batteries in BAOR and a few towed pieces for air-portable use around the world. In November 1963 the United States was reported as being utterly uninterested in unguided rockets due to them not seeing any possibilities in the concept. Germany, however, was interested. Germany had recently introduced the 110mm Light Artillery Rocket (LAR) and was looking at a Medium Artillery Rocket (MAR). The German work was under way in 1964, and by 1967 the British saw it as a good idea to begin discussions with Germany about a joint project. These discussions started in January 1970 and lasted throughout the year. Italy also expressed an interest in the final solution, whatever it may be. At the first meeting, all three countries laid out their current progress in rocket artillery and ideas and aims.

Italy had been working on three projects named the ARCO, ARTIGLIO and Breda 51 GS. The first two were designed by SNIA Viscosa-BPD and were cancelled for technological reasons. The Breda 51 was a 152mm rocket with a 35kg warhead and a range of 23km. The Italians saw that it was below the NATO standards laid out in NMBR 39. This latter standard was for the non-nuclear destruction of hard targets by indirect gunfire. It included full standardization details for the 155mm artillery, which would result in the attempt at standardization to the failed SP70, and laid out some rough figures for a rocket solution, although the latter was not fully detailed. Because the Breda 51 was unable to meet these requirements, it was being used as a test and development chassis.

Italy did have one other rocket under development: this was the RC12, produced as a private venture by OTO-Melara and SNIA Viscosa-BPD. The Italian government had no official interest in this rocket, but it was included in their briefing for the sake of completeness. Based on a 105/14 howitzer, it came in two versions with a lighter steel version weighing 45kg or a cast-iron one weighing 48kg. The warheads weighed 19kg and 22kg respectively. The range was 15 to 16km depending on which type of warhead was used. The RC12 carriage came in two versions, a single or a twelve-rail launcher with a rate of fire of one rocket every 0.5 seconds.

Germany's MAR programme was able to reach the requirements laid out by NATO. They took a different approach to Britain and had decided on a cheaper rocket that would reach 60km. This design would mount a warhead that could deploy a scatterable minefield, which would neutralize and halt enemy movements for a limited period. These scatterable minefields were of a larger area effect than the British warheads and so needed less accuracy to include the target within their footprint. The simpler German rockets were predicted to cost about one-third of a similar British rocket. One example of the differences was that the Germans canted the fins on their design to spin the rocket to counter-thrust misalignment.

The German warheads were also described. At the time, there were four types planned. The first was a cluster bomb version, with fifty 35mm submunitions, each weighing 250 grams. These gave a penetration of 160mm. Each bomblet had been optimized to produce 600 fragments on detonation, which were lethal out to 5m.

The next three warhead options were all named, possibly by the company Messerschmitt-Bölkow-Blohm (MBB) which was working on developing them. 'Pandora' was the first warhead; it contained eight quadrant-shaped bar mines, each 300mm long and 60mm tall. They held 950g of explosive and were fitted with an anti-lift device and a self-destruct timer. 'Medusa' was an anti-tank mine. The warhead held five two-directional HEAT mines. This design meant that no matter which way up the mine landed, one of the two HEAT cones would be facing upwards. Each mine contained 1kg of explosive, was 120mm tall and was detonated by a magnetic sensor, which would only trip when an armoured vehicle crossed above it. *Drachensaat* ('Dragon's teeth', i.e. 'seeds of discord') was another anti-infantry warhead. It contained fifty-six submunitions. The submunition was 80mm long, although they needed to land a certain way up and thus required stabilization, which increased the length to 150mm. After impacting, the mines would lay dormant until each submunition would activate, at which point the mine would bounce into the air and explode at a height of 2m. Each submunition contained more than 1,000 spheres, each just 2.15mm across. The random nature of these detonations and the extreme lethality would render an area of 600sqm uncrossable to infantry for the hour that the delay timer was functioning.

At this first meeting, due to the Germans sticking to their requirements of 60km range and minelets, the British yielded to German pressure and signed up to carry out an investigation into increasing Foil's reach out to that distance and a suitable warhead. From that starting-point, all three countries agreed to hold further talks on creating a standardized requirement and shared equipment.

During 1970 the Foil investigation continued and a calibre of 10.4in was selected as being suitable for the German requirements. While progress had been made in this field, the propellant was now proving more problematic. First, the burn rate and pressures were very different. The British rockets had a 36mm per second burn rate and a combustion chamber pressure of 280 bars, which launched the rocket at 90g. Germany, on the other hand, insisted on a rocket with a 15mm per second burn rate, giving 120 bars and just 30g. In the end, a compromise burn rate of 25mm per second and 196 bars was reached.

Equally the Germans were insisting on a very low temperature of operation of –40 degrees. At that time –31 degrees was the lowest

A LARS-1 taking part in the celebration parade for twenty years of NATO. This was held in the Nürburgring on 6 June 1969.

temperature at which the British propellant could be used. Britain pointed out that they never tested equipment below –31 unless the GSR required it. This procedure was in line with STANAG agreements on temperature. It is described in some British reports as the 1 per cent value, or a temperature not exceeded for more than 1 per cent of the year, or about three or four days. The Germans, on the other hand, were insisting on temperatures based on meteorological data indicating the coldest ever temperatures recorded over the previous fifty years across all of Germany, including mountains. This was seen as an excuse not to take up British equipment due to the Germans accepting –31 degrees operating temperature for the SPH-70

155mm howitzer, which had a hull based upon the Leopard 1 MBT. The same chassis was to be used for the new rocket family, with a launcher not exceeding 10 tons in weight, and the total weight of the vehicle not exceeding 37.5 tons. Wegmann undertook the study into the launcher.

Eventually, the projects would result in the RS-80, which the British also called Foil. During the early 1970s, the rift between Germany and the UK over the core issue of accuracy and costs continued to grow.

In March 1972 the Defence Operational Analysis Establishment (DOAE) concluded a series of computer simulations into RS-80. These studies had been running since 1970, and had covered the British Foil and then matured to include the RS-80. These studies considered the effect of adding four rocket batteries to BAOR and how effective they would be at destroying enemy tanks. The effectiveness of the four batteries was compared to spending either the equivalent financial or manpower costs on Chieftain tanks or SPH-70 batteries firing cluster munitions. The Chieftain option included adding another Chieftain per troop, and another armoured regiment to the BAOR order of battle. Additional SPH-70 batteries would be four more than currently planned for manpower or a whopping twelve more batteries for the same financial cost.

The results across all the studies were the same. Even with a degree of bias and weighting in the calculations in the rocket batteries' favour, unless the Soviets packed their vehicles in very close to each other, the rockets were less efficient than the other solutions at killing tanks. It was pointed out, on several occasions, against APCs and artillery targets, a rocket using a PFF warhead would be massively cheaper and more efficient and very lethal. However, the primary focus of the study was cluster warheads against tanks.

It might seem odd to compare indirect fire against direct fire in the case of the Chieftains, but this was explained away by the simple problem of finding and acquiring targets beyond the forward edge of battle. At the time no long-range surveillance technology could be relied upon to aim these weapons out to their maximum range without a long delay time of about thirty minutes, by which time the target was likely to have moved. This delay negatively affected the ability of the rockets to bring effective fire onto the tank formations. Again artillery-locating radar was seen as a quick and efficient solution to solving this against enemy artillery. Such a device as the ZENDA radar just entering service linked to a Foil battery could report the location of a Soviet artillery battery in seconds.

A very grainy image of a Federal Republic of Germany LARS-1 launcher in action as it fires one of its eighteen 110mm rockets.

Then a Foil battery could launch a battery salvo of PFF and displace instantly to a new position, at which point they could reload. Using a combination of tactics would rapidly diminish, if not eliminate, Soviet artillery support.

With the DOAE report citing that RS-80 would be an expensive and inefficient system and the continuing problems in coming to an agreement with Germany, Britain finally withdrew from the RS-80 project in 1975. The project would continue for several years with both the Italians and Germans working on it. However, the NATO requirement NMBR 39 contained one key stipulation: the ability to bulk-reload. Neither the British Foil nor the RS-80 could reload its rockets in bulk. About the same time that Britain withdrew from the RS-80 programme, the United States reviewed its stance on rocket artillery and started a development programme that would result in the M270 MLRS, which very rapidly became the standard rocket-launcher for NATO. Sometimes called the Self-Propelled Loader/Launcher (SPLL), the system's ability to reload six rockets as a single pod revolutionized the way in which the West looked at rocket artillery and met all of the NMBR 39 requirements.

Sources

	Bovington Tank Museum	The National Archives
PART ONE	• 1984.198.161 A45 loading with stabilized gun • 2005.1765 Centurion with A45 bridge mock-up • 2009.2703 FV201 liaison letter • 2011.1667 Vickers tanks notes • 2014.147 US ammo in 120mm L1 • 2014.627 Misc FV221 • 2014.631 The Universal Tank • 2014.638 Provisional sketch • 2014.641 Details of .30 cal in A45 turret • 2014.643 FV201 plans • 2014.645 A45 mine attack • 2014.646 A45 AVRE • 2014.649 details of improvements of A45 over Centurion • 2014.650 The Universal Tank narrative • 2014.651 New pitch track • 2014.653 FV201 ammo loading • 2014.747 Misc FV221 • 2014.1372 • 2014.1429 FV214 track-throwing trials • 2014.1524 motion study loading FV214	• AVIA 65/453 Claim by William Beardmore's • DEFE 15/1102 Armament for MT-2 possible solutions • DEFE 15/1901 Liquid propellant guns. Report 1, 1954 • DEFE 15/1906 Liquid propellant guns. Report 4, 1956 • DEFE 15/1919 Liquid propellant 90mm Detroit gun • SUPP 6/484 Ordnance board proceedings • W0 32/16607 New gun for MT2 • WO 32/12086 Long-Range Flame-thrower for medium tanks • WO 32/12087 The Universal Tank • WO 32/15322 New Main Battle Tank development • WO 185/292 Tanks: TV 200 Series: policy and design • WO 185/293 FV215 file • WO 185/384 Design and development of MT4201 and 4202

	Bovington Tank Museum	**The National Archives**
	• 2014.3497 CIRD vibrator device • 2014.3738 Flail beating pattern • E2011.1890 RAC development reports 1951 • E2011.2889 RAC development reports 1952 • E2011.2891 RAC development reports 1951 • E2011.2892 RAC development reports 1951 • E2011.2893 RAC development reports 1953 • E2011.2896 RAC development reports 1955 • E2011.2897 RAC development reports 1956 • E2011.2901 RAC development reports 1957 • E2011.2907 RAC development reports 1958 • E2011.2909 RAC development reports 1959	• WO 194/390 Chieftain mantlet trials • WO 194/1580 Comparative trials of 6.5 inch and 7.5 inch guns in Churchill Armoured Vehicles, Royal Engineers (AVREs) • WO 194/1597 Further trials with 6.5 inch gun in Armoured Vehicle, Royal Engineers (AVRE) • WO 195/13225 Armament for MT-2 • WO 286/75 Development of new round for 165mm Armoured Vehicle, Royal Engineers, High-Explosive Squash Head x 3 series • WO 286/76 Development of new round for 165mm (AVRE), HESH X3 series • WO 291/1060 A45 Flame guns versus the *Panzerfaust* weapon • WW 291/1071 Motion study of loading 6.5 inch
RAC conference notes	• 1963.50.15 • 2004.3652 • 2004.3656 • 2004.3658 • 2004.3661 • 2004.3662 • 2005.319 • 2005.320 • 2005.330 • 2005.332 • 2005.333 • 2005.334 • 2005.335 • 2005.336 • 2005.1546 • 2012.447	• WO 341/74 • WO 341/75 • WO 341/89 • WO 341/90 • WO 341/91

	Bovington Tank Museum	**The National Archives**
PART TWO	• 623.438.4 Development report 11, FV4401 Contentious • 2013.2395 Prodigal • Limited airborne ability • Project C • Suggested future weapon systems for Royal Armoured Corps use, inc. US Shillelagh	• BT 268/11 Stage 1 report on P-35 • DEFE 4/182 Close-Support Light Weapons system • DEFE 15/1180 GSOR 1012 Interim report • DEFE 15/1214 Prodigal, some initial designs for automatic feed systems • DEFE 15/1940 GSOR 1012 Possible solutions • WO 32/18926 Ground-effect machines • WO 32/19912 War Office Policy Statement: No 2, Armoured Reconnaissance Vehicles • WO 32/20037 Ground-Air Vehicles • WO 32/20044 Ground-Air Vehicles development and production • WO 194-1565 General Staff Requirement – GSR 3301 Feasibility study Armoured Vehicle Reconnaissance • WO 194/344 The performance of cast ribbed armour • WO 194/935 Performance of ribbed armour • WO 194/1351 Contentious briefing to US • WO 194/1564 GSOR 1010 Possible solutions • WO 194/1565 GSOR 3301 Feasibility study Armoured Vehicle Reconnaissance • WO 194/1567 GST 31 The case for tracked close-support weapon system • WO 194/1579 GST 31 The case for tracked close-support weapon system

SOURCES

	Bovington Tank Museum	**The National Archives**
PART THREE	• 2015.2145 FV401 Water performance trials • 2015.2149 FV401 Carrier development trials • 2015.2151 FV401 Carriage of 120mm ammunition • 2015.2165 FV401 Armour proving trials • 2015.2419 FV401 Carrier development trials • Carrier, Universal, FV401	• AIR 66/20 Oxford loading trials • DEFE 70/19 Misc cannon options • WO 20/8273 APC regiments • WO 32/11854 Employment of infantry and APCs • WO 32/21239 APC weapon system development • WO 194/712 RR close-support carrier CT24
PART FOUR	• Carrier, tracked, launcher, Orange William, FV426	• AVIA 54/1779 Australian Anti-Tank Project • AVIA 65/2233 Swingfire history • BT 268/151 Swingfire on SR.N6 • DEFE 15/2286 Swingfire hang fire • DEFE 48/508 Foil in the anti-tank role • WO 29/20097 Project JAWL • WO 32/20041 Swingfire misc • WO 32/21698 GB/IT/GER discussions on Foil • WO 194/1356 Foil Phase 1
	Historical Archives of the Hungarian State Security • ref. 3.2.2. T/9-1	

Several archives provided material for this work, free of charge, and do not endorse this publication in any way. These organizations are The National Archives of Australia, Great Britain and Hungary, as well as Das Bundesarchiv and the Imperial War Museum.

Index

Foil (Project), 175, 177–80, 182,
  184–5

Girling, 12
GSOR
  1001, 101
  1006, 101
  1007, 165
  1009, 92
  1010, 101–106, 109–10, 112–13
  1012, 101, 104
  1013, 164, 171
  1016, 87
  1105, 136
  1174, 166
  3038, 112, 116, 118–22
  3165, 138
  3301, 112–16, 120, 123–5
GSR
  3340, 125
GST
  17, 173, 177
  3019, 177
Guns, Recoilless Rifles and
  Cannon, American
  M139 20mm (see also VRFWS
    and HS820), 104
  M191A5 .30 cal machine gun, 21
  T122 120mm, 54
  T123 120mm, 54
  T53 120mm, 54
  TRW 6425, 102, 139–141
Guns, Recoilless Rifles and
  Cannon, British
  105mm experimental, 5, 66
  105mm Light Gun, 116–18
  17–pounder, 4, 18, 30, 64, 78,
    84, 87, 133

180mm Lillywhite, 59
20–pounder, 7, 14–16, 18, 34,
  45, 53, 64–6, 68, 80
25–pounder, 2, 14, 36, 84–5,
  134, 174
2–pounder, 64, 68, 82
3.7in Heavy AA gun, 4–5, 14, 174
30mm ADEN Gun, 82
4.5in experimental tank gun, 8,
  14–15, 45
6–pounder, 83
6.5in, 7, 22–6, 59
7.5in Jeffries gun, 22–3
L1 120mm gun, 50, 53–7, 84
L11 120mm gun, 66, 87, 166
L21 30mm RARDEN, 105–
  106, 108, 112, 115, 140–2
L4 183mm, 59–60, 63, 153
L5 76mm gun, 104, 108
L6 120mm WOMBAT, 108,
  118, 138, 165
L60 40mm Bofors, 104
L7 105mm gun, 57, 66, 87
L70 40mm Bofors, 104
Polsten 20mm, 4
Tankard 50mm, 103
Guns, Recoilless Rifles and
  Cannon, German
  HS820 20mm, 139–41
Guns, Recoilless Rifles and
  Cannon, Soviet
  12.7mm, 107, 138
  BS–3 100mm, 52
  D10T 100mm, 52

Handley Page Ltd, 95
Harding, Lieutenant Colonel
  John, 135